JUNG AND
THE CHRISTIAN WAY

JUNG AND
THE CHRISTIAN WAY

Christopher Bryant

The Seabury Press

Originally published in 1983 in Great Britain by
Darton, Longman and Todd Ltd.
Library of Congress Catalog Card Number: 84-51075
ISBN: 0-86683-872-4
Printed in the United States of America
5   4   3   2   1

The Seabury Press
430 Oak Grove
Minneapolis, Minnesota 55403

CONTENTS

ACKNOWLEDGMENT

Thanks are due to the following for permission to reproduce material from copyright sources:

Princeton University Press: The Collected Works of C. G. Jung: vol. VI *Psychological Types* 1971; vol. VII *Two Essays on Analytical Psychology* 1953; vol. VIII *The Structure and Dynamics of the Psyche* 1960; vol. X *Civilization in Transition* 1964; vol XI *Psychology and Religion: West and East* 1958; vol. XV *The Spirit of Man* 1967; vol. XVI *The Practice of Psychotherapy* 1954.

INTRODUCTION

The immediate origin of this book is a series of six lectures on Jung and Christianity which I gave in 1980 at the invitation of the then vicar, the late David Sparrow, in the church of All Saints, Margaret Street, London. I was grateful for the opportunity the lectures gave me of thinking out and sharing with others some of the insights I have gained from the great Swiss psychologist. I am grateful also to my publishers, Darton, Longman and Todd, for their encouraging me to expand the lectures into a book and so reach a larger public.

I feel indebted to Jung for the light he has shed for me on the Christian faith and way of life; and I hope this book may do something to discharge the debt. Jung himself believed that he had much to offer theologians and pastors in their task of interpreting the Christian gospel to men and women of the twentieth century; and he was surprised and disappointed that only a comparative few of them paid serious attention to his work. Since his death Christian thinkers have come increasingly to recognize Jung's greatness and the spiritual relevance of his exploration of the human psyche.

The aim of this book is twofold. First I hope to convince Christian readers, who know little or nothing about Jung, of his relevance; that he can help them to understand their faith and live their life as Christians better. This has meant that I have had to give some outline of Jung's ideas. I have however made no attempt to provide a complete account of his thought and writings, a task for which I am in no way competent. What I offer is an impressionistic sketch of those elements of his teaching which have helped me and, I think, are especially relevant to Christians today. The Jungian expert, if he chances to read this book, may well take exception not only to actual errors which I have inadvertently committed or subtleties that I have ignored but also to particular interpretations of Jungian ideas and themes. Jung is a seminal thinker who is deeply concerned to bring order into the dense and largely unknown jungle of psychic reality and throws out exploratory paths for those who will to follow. I have chosen to follow one path, the path which connects with regions which have been partly charted by Christian spiritual writers of the past. I cannot suppose that Jung would have agreed with all that I have written, but I believe he would have heartily approved my attempt to follow up his ideas.

The second aim of this book is to persuade those who are already acquainted with the thought and writings of Jung but who have repudiated Christianity or regarded it as irrelevant to their needs to take another look at it. William Johnston has interestingly described a dialogue between Christians and Buddhists in Japan: 'We found that dialogue based on theology and philosophy did not achieve much; but when we talked from experience we suddenly discovered how closely united we really were.'[1] I believe that, though the conceptual worlds of Jungian psychology and Christianity appear to be alien to each other, the experience underlying the concepts is similar. I believe that many who through Jung have learnt to make real contact with their own depths would find without surrendering their Jungian insights an enlargement and enrichment of them through Christian worship and prayer. The Christianity I have in mind is a way of prayer and worship rather than an ecclesiastical or doctrinal system.

It is perhaps presumptuous of me to write about Jung at all. For I have never undergone a Jungian analysis or been in a position to study Jung in the depth required, and probably lack the mental equipment for such study. But it seems to me that I have something that demands to be shared with

---

1 *Silent Music* (Collins 1974), p. 9

others and this I attempt to do. As a theological student I
became acquainted with Jung as one of the great triumvirate
of depth psychologists, Freud, Jung and Adler. But it was the
reading of Jung's *Modern Man in Search of a Soul* some ten years
later that for the first time fully aroused my interest in him.
My first reaction was one of fascination mingled with misgiv-
ing. I was attracted by the authority and depth of his description of human experience; but I had misgivings about the
compatibility of his psychology with Christian belief. My
doubts were laid to rest partly by the occasional articles and
reviews of the distinguished Dominican theologian, Victor
White, which appeared from time to time in the monthly
Blackfriars journal, and later by his books, *God and the Unconscious* and *Soul and Psyche*. Another book which greatly helped
me to relate Jungian with Christian teaching was *Jung and St
Paul* by the Reverend David Cox. Later still I found much to
stimulate my thinking in the writings of Harry Williams and
in particular *The True Wilderness*. With an enviably clear and
lively literary style and a complete freedom from psychological jargon he shows unmistakably the influence of Jung. One
other very important help to my understanding of Jung and
his contemporary relevance came from my membership in a
small group, the hard core of which consisted of some five
Jungian-trained analysts and three clergy. For about six years
we used to meet four or five times a year to talk over matters
of common concern, theological, pastoral and psychological.
This group more than any other influence has enabled me
to articulate ideas ranging over the large territory in which
psychology, psychotherapy and both pastoral and spiritual
theology stake a claim. Talking and writing about the
interrelationship of theology and psychology has brought clarity into my thinking about this frontier area. Further, in the
work of giving spiritual guidance to others I have found in
the ideas of Jung a set of valuable tools for exploring the
mystery which confronts us in every man and woman. I must
however confess that I have seldom found a direct road from
the study of psychology to the understanding of other people.
It has only been as psychology deepened and extended my
own self-awareness that it has enabled me to understand
others. It is only as I have come to recognize my own largely

unconscious fear and aggression that I have been able to sense and to understand similar emotions in others.

I never had the opportunity of meeting Jung nor did it even occur to me that I might correspond with him as some of my friends did. But I have been reading his writings sporadically over the past forty years, and there has been a continuing dialogue in my own mind with the thought of one whom I regard as one of the great men of our times. This book is the fruit of that inner dialogue.

Readers will discover that in the later chapters of the book I often summarize or restate ideas and themes dealt with earlier. This reiteration and repetition of points already made is partly due to the fact that the original lectures, which were given at fortnightly intervals, required me to do a lot of recapitulating and summarizing if my hearers were to gain some intelligent grasp and conspectus of the course as a whole. But I have deliberately refrained from eliminating altogether this element of recapitulation and reaffirmation. For I have found that the psychic realities of which Jung writes are elusive and cannot be grasped quickly; they need to be pondered and, like some great mountain, looked at from a number of angles before their meaning can be assimilated.

I have to thank Baroness Vera von der Heydt, the Reverend David Cox and Mr David Black for kindly reading the original lectures in typescript and for their helpful criticisms and suggestions. My thanks are also due to Miss Lesley Riddle of Darton, Longman and Todd for encouragement and practical comments, and for the criticisms of two of the firm's readers from which I have profited greatly.

June 1982   Christopher Bryant

1

JUNG AND RELIGION

In a television interview on the BBC which Jung gave shortly before he died in 1961 his interviewer, John Freeman, asked him if he believed in God. 'I don't need to believe, I know,' was Jung's reply. For him God was a tremendous and awe-inspiring experience. Some of Jung's unorthodox statements about religion have aroused the hostile criticisms of theologians, but there can be no question as to the importance Jung ascribed to the experience of God. He believed that many of the ills of the modern world were due to its being cut off from its religious roots.

(i)

Born in 1875 Carl Jung was cradled in religion. The son of a Swiss Protestant pastor and of a mother all of whose six brothers were clergymen, he had throughout his life an absorbing interest in religion. Writing in old age he recalled that at the age of fifteen 'nobody could rid me of the conviction that it was enjoined upon me to do what God wanted, not what I wanted. That gave me strength to go my own way. Often I had the feeling that in all decisive matters I was no longer among men but was alone with God.'[1] He said of

1   *Memories, Dreams and Reflections* (Pantheon 1977) p. 65

himself at a later age, 'I find that all my thoughts circle round God, like the planets round the sun, and are as irresistibly attracted by him. I would feel it to be the grossest sin if I were to oppose any resistance to this force.'[2] But religious though he was he came to be suspicious of the religious ideas and beliefs in which he had been brought up. It seemed to him that much of the religion that was practised in his father's church was a sham, a kind of make-believe. The churchgoers had no real conviction of the truth of the words they said or sang; there was no living experience behind them. He writes with compassion of his father who could not bring himself to face the doubts which were slowly undermining his faith, doubts which in all probability contributed to his mental breakdown and premature death. When asked questions about doctrine his father was apt to put him off with, 'You must have faith'. His father knew nothing of a religious experience which might have validated and vivified his faith. Jung tells us of an incident causing him acute disappointment when his father was preparing him for confirmation. His father's instructions were based on a catechism. The young Carl looking ahead at the syllabus waited impatiently for the time when they would reach the section dealing with the doctrine of the Trinity, which fascinated him. When at last the point was reached his father said, 'We will pass over this section; it is not important, and I can make nothing of it myself.' With that remark the boy's hopes were dashed to the ground and he lost all further interest in the course of instruction.

All his life Jung was concerned with knowing God, with the immediate intuitive awareness of God. He believed that the religion of many Christians who, like his father, relied on an intellectual faith, divorced from any experience of the realities believed in, was seriously defective. In a letter written in 1945 at the age of seventy he affirms, '*It is of the highest importance* that the educated and "enlightened" should know religious truth as a thing living in the human soul and not as an abstruse and unreasonable relic of the past.'[3] With the

2   Ibid., p. 13
3   *Letters*, vol. i, p. 387

growth of secularism and the weakening of the authority both of the Bible and of Christian tradition there is a growing recognition that faith is much more than intellectual belief and must involve commitment of the whole person and should include at least some intuition of God. Jung however was not a theologian and when he speaks disparagingly of faith it is this intellectual belief that he has in mind. He regularly contrasts faith with experiential knowledge, as in his reply to John Freeman's question, whereas the experience of God should properly be understood as one element in a mature faith.

Jung was highly critical of the general run of theologians for being out of touch with the needs of men and women in the contemporary world. He thought their attitude too cerebral. They were too concerned in his opinion with trying to prove the existence of God and not concerned enough with helping people to realize God in their experience. He says of them:

> With a truly tragic delusion these theologians fail to see that it is not a matter of theologians proving the existence of light but of blind people who do not know that their eyes could see. It is high time that we realized that it is pointless to praise the light if nobody can see it. It is much more needful to teach people the art of seeing.[4]

It is here I think that Jung can help the Christian today, to an awareness of the all-encompassing reality of God. For it is clear that the reason why many moderns neglect or ignore religious truth is not so much because it is thought to be untrue as because, true or false, it is felt to be irrelevant, that it does not work in practice and has no real bearing on life as it is actually lived. Jung produces a mass of evidence to show that religion does work and that it can act as a transforming and renewing influence in those who will open themselves to its influence.

It was because Jung was a profoundly religious man that he was able to shed a new and brilliant light on the whole field of religious psychology. Professor G. S. Spinks in no way

---

4 *Psychology and Alchemy.* Quoted by Raymond Hostie, *Religion and the Psychology of Jung* (Sheed and Ward 1957), p. 171

exaggerates, in my opinion, when he writes that Jung's contribution to religious psychology exceeds that of any other writer of this century.[5] As with all great thinkers his ideas changed and developed; only gradually did his theoretical formulations take shape. The development of his thought cannot be understood without some reference to his relationship with Sigmund Freud, the great pioneer of depth psychology. Before ever he met Freud, Jung as a young doctor on the staff of the Burgholzli, an important Swiss mental hospital, had made a name for himself through his contributions to medical journals. Jung became deeply interested in the work of the Viennese psychologist, an older man by some twenty years, which corroborated certain discoveries of his own. In 1907 he visited Freud in Vienna for the first time. The interest of the two men in this their first meeting can be gauged by the fact that beginning at 1 p.m. they continued talking with virtually no break for thirteen hours. An intimate friendship sprang up between them and for six years Jung collaborated with Freud in producing a psychological journal which the younger man edited. But, despite his admiration for Freud's pioneer work, from the first he had reservations about the key place of sexuality in Freud's psychological system. It is true that Freud defines sexuality very broadly. He distinguishes between affective and genital sexuality, the latter being only one, though a biologically very important, form in which sexuality expresses itself. He regards as sexual the infant's intense attachment to mother and father and indeed all affectionate relationships. He regards the drive which impels men to construct civilization and build empires as well as the urge to artistic creation and the religious impulse as disguised and sublimated sexuality. Jung agreed with Freud that sex played a large and greatly underestimated part in human lives but he could not accept that it accounted for practically everything. And so as Jung has written: 'When Freud publicly declared that psycho-analysis and his sexual theory were indissolubly wedded, I was obliged to strike out on a different path.'[6]

5   G. S. Spinks, *Psychology and Religion* (Methuen 1963), p. 90
6   Quoted Hostie, op. cit., p. 25

Though Jung spoke critically of the limitations of Freud's sexual theory he always spoke with respect of the man. He regarded him as a kind of prophet who saw it as his mission to strip the veil of hypocrisy from much nineteenth-century idealism. 'All the gush', he writes, 'about man's innate goodness, which had addled so many brains after the dogma of original sin was no longer understood, was blown to the winds by Freud.'[7] As a destroyer of cant and idealistic make-believe Freud was the liberator of a whole generation.

Jung was not the only one-time follower and collaborator who broke away from Freud on the issue of his sexual theory. Before Jung's breach Alfred Adler had cut adrift for the same reason and founded his own school of individual psychology. Adler saw the instinct of self-preservation and the urge for power as the most fundamental of human instinctive drives. He understood neuroses not, like Freud, as caused by the frustration of the sex drive but as due to the block of the will to power. Jung for his part accepted the importance both of the sex drive and of the will to power. He writes:

It would be an unpardonable error to overlook the element of truth in both the Freudian and Adlerian viewpoints, but it would be no less unpardonable to take either of them as the sole truth. Both truths correspond to psychological realities. There are in fact some cases which by and large can best be described and explained by the one theory and some by the other . . . It seems hardly necessary to add that I hold the truth of my own deviationist views to be equally relative.[8]

He also writes:

The more deeply we penetrate the nature of the psyche the more the conviction grows upon us that the diversity, the multi-dimensionality of human nature requires the greatest variety of standpoints and methods in order to satisfy the variety of psychic dispositions.

Jung, while accepting as we have seen the limited validity of

7 *Collected Works* (Princeton), vol. xv, p. 46
8 *C. W.*, vol. xvi, paras 68 and 70

the points of view of both Freud and Adler, believed that the psychological facts could be better explained if the libido or psychic energy were understood neither as sex drive nor as will to power but as undifferentiated energy. This energy might flow predominantly either along the sex channel or along that of the will to power; but at bottom it was seeking an end other than that of either of these powerful drives. The nature of this psychic energy is best understood by looking at its goal, man or woman fully developed. You understand the nature of an acorn less by studying its chemical composition or investigating the manner in which the young sapling copes with its environmental hazards than by contemplating the full-grown oak tree that the acorn has it in it to become. So in Jung's view the psychic energy in each individual presses him from his earliest years to realize his innate capacities to the fullest possible extent, to live out his own individual truth, to achieve what Jung calls individuation. The systems of Freud and Adler were especially valuable for dealing with things that had gone wrong in the acorn stage or the period soon after its planting, that is the period of infancy and childhood, when the individual lives his life under the care of parents. It is sometimes essential for progress first of all to go back and with expert psychotherapeutic help untie some of the strings which got knotted during this early period. A large part of the work of psychotherapists is concerned with unblocking channels clogged up in infancy and early childhood; and they are likely to find the views of Freud and Adler and their successors of especial value. Jung's own particular interest and concern however was with the neuroses which occurred in middle life to men and women who had largely overcome these early problems. He was interested too in the central part which religion played in the healing of these older persons.

(ii)

But before considering Jung's ideas of religion and its therapeutic importance it is necessary to look at a certain agnosticism which has disturbed some Christian readers of his writings. Though Jung has never denied the existence of God and has constantly affirmed the immense human value of religion he sometimes writes as though the God-experience is all-important whether or not it is an experience of the living God whom Christians, Jews and Moslems believe in. Some of Jung's followers have rejected the objective existence of God and understood the God-experience as being merely the vivid awareness of the depth and vastness of the human psyche. Father Raymond Hostie in his study of Jung[9] argues that Jung's earlier writings show him to be agnostic as to God's existence. Though deeply interested in religion and affirming against Freud its unique value for mankind he was not prepared to commit himself to the objective reality of God. This was partly due to the agnostic atmosphere of the scientific circles in which he moved. It was partly due to his adherence to the philosophical position of Immanuel Kant, that we can know nothing at all about what things are in themselves; all we can know is the phenomena, the appearances; the reality behind the appearances is completely unknown to us. Perhaps an even more pressing reason for his agnostic attitude was his determination to establish his psychology on a scientific and therefore an empirical basis. He wanted to study and so far as possible understand the workings of the human psyche without the interference of philosophy or theology; particularly of theology with its inveterate tendency to dogmatize and prescribe what must be the case without regard to the observed facts of the psyche.

If Hostie is right Jung went through an agnostic phase in which he was heavily criticized from two opposite points of view. He was criticized by theologians who regarded him as an atheist, like Freud, and saw his psychology as offering a means of accounting for religion without the existence of God. On the other hand he was criticized by psychologists as a believer who manipulated the psychic facts in the interests of theistic belief. It was the attack by his fellow psychologists who called in question his scientific integrity to which Jung was most vulnerable. It may have been due to this that he maintained an agnostic attitude. But he was also hurt by the

9 Hostie, op. cit.

hostile criticism of theologians who, he thought, should have welcomed the evidence he brought forward of the profound human importance of religion. According to Hostie he came through this agnostic phase in the 1930s. The change was brought about partly as a result of his researches into the period when Christianity captured the imagination of the Roman world and, even more, as a result of his therapeutic work with his patients. He came increasingly to realize the healing and life-enhancing power of religion. He always maintained that psychology cannot prove the existence of God, nor indeed disprove it. Nor could the God-experience prove that God exists, though of course it provided important evidence which the philosopher must take into account. But speaking as a human being and not as a psychologist he admitted that he himself believed in God. In a conversation with Hostie Jung once remarked: 'It is quite clear that God exists, but why are people always asking me to prove this psychologically?'[10] In a letter written in 1950 Jung refers to a writer who speaks of the God-image in man as the door through which he finds God and says:

> I can only concur with this view, but with the best will in the world I cannot maintain that this is a verifiable assertion, which is what science is about. It is a subjective assertion which has no place in science.[11, 12]

From an orthodox Christian standpoint I find Jung's attitude to belief less than satisfactory, though entirely understandable and perhaps in the circumstances the only possible one for him to take. For the impression I gain especially from his letters is that, while accepting the existence of God as an opinion which, though highly probable, cannot be scientifi-

10 Hostie, op. cit., p. 160n
11 Jung, *Letters*, vol. i, p. 556
12 It is necessary to state that Jung was highly critical of Hostie's book on the grounds that Hostie had misinterpreted his psychological language as philosophical; words which attempted to indicate psychic facts were treated as ontological statements and criticized accordingly (see Jung, *Letters*, vol. ii, p. 244). Whether or not Jung is quite fair to Hostie, I do not see that his criticism necessarily falsifies the substantial accuracy of Hostie's account of the agnostic phase through which he thinks Jung passed.

cally proved, he does not regard belief as important. He does not need to believe, he knows. Jung expresses his strong reaction against a purely intellectual belief, the belief in God's existence together with certain propositions about him, divorced from any experience of God. In this he is surely right. Faith involves much more than belief in God's existence and certain revealed truths about him. The experience of God which is all-important for Jung is an essential element in a mature Christian faith. The New Testament itself witnesses to a new and life-changing experience of God, mediated through Jesus, the Messiah. But if faith is more than bare belief it must include it as the New Testament itself bears witness. A full faith means the commitment of the whole person including the intellect to the reality of God, even though that reality cannot be scientifically proved. Faith involves an individual in an intellectual venture, it leads him to embark on a voyage of discovery, as he tries to understand the people and the happenings around him in the light of his belief in God; only the voyage itself can confirm the faith with which he sets out. If God exists certain other truths and possibilities flow from this primary truth. If God exists he is concerned not only for me but for all men and women, indeed for the whole universe. He is not only the central point of my own life; he is also the still point of the turning world. I believe that Jung was wholly committed to God as he grasped him in his own experience; but one man's experience is inevitably limited and needs to be complemented by the experience of mankind. If God exists the possibility that he has revealed himself and his will for mankind must be taken seriously; and that the human search for God may be a blind response to God's prior disclosure of himself in a thousand ways. It seems to me that Jung's disregard of the importance of intellectual belief is as one-sided as the disregard of the importance of religious experience which he attacks. I believe that Jung is destined to play an important part in the revival of Christian faith among educated men and women of the West. but his role will be more that of a John the Baptist who prepared the way for the coming of Christ than that of one of Christ's apostles.

Associated with Jung's underestimate of the importance of

belief is his practice of using the word 'God' ambiguously, sometimes to refer to God himself, sometimes to the human idea of God. Thus in his *Answer to Job* he refers to the changing and maturing of the human conception of God as the changing and maturing of God. Jung was perfectly clear himself as to the distinction between God and the changing and developing human ideas about him. But it is quite understandable that Christian readers should have misunderstood him and found the book offensive.

Another accusation that Jung had to face was that his theories were an elaborate construction inadequately based on fact. In part this was the criticism that experimental psychology brought against all the schools of depth psychology, Freud and Adler no less than Jung. Jung's reply was that he was concerned to understand human life as it was actually lived and not merely the small fragments of life which the experimental psychologist isolated and measured in the controlled and highly artificial conditions of the psychological laboratory or deduced from the analysis of statistics or the study of animal behaviour. In the face of criticism Jung insisted that his psychology was empirically based and scientific, because founded on psychological facts which were none the less real for being hard to measure and map. He regarded his theories as tools by means of which he sought to bring some order out of the forest of psychological phenomena. He did not regard his theories – of the self or of archetypes, for example – as absolute truths but as useful instruments for exploring the human psyche. In 1951 at the age of 76 he wrote:

> Our psychological experience is too recent and too limited in scope to permit of general theories. The investigator needs a lot more facts which would throw light on the nature of the psyche before he can begin to think of universally valid propositions.[13]

Jung was like one of the early cartographers doing his best to construct a map of Africa, incorporating the information he has received from reasonably reliable sources, but well aware

13 Quoted Hostie, op. cit., p. 8

that he had not nearly enough accurate data for a fully reliable map. Speaking of his ideas about the structure of the soul he writes:

> There is no question of my producing incontrovertible truths – they are simply ideas thrown out in an attempt to bring a bit of order into the bewildering conglomeration of psychic realities.[14]

When someone disagreed with one of his hypotheses Jung expected him to produce another which would explain the phenomena more simply, without ignoring or explaining away any of the psychological facts. He regarded all his theories as provisional until a better theory should be produced.

Jung makes a distinction, likely to prove disconcerting if not understood, between psychological truth and objective or absolute truth. Something may be psychologically real but objectively false. If a person suffers from the delusion that he has cancer while medical examination proves that he has not, his delusion is a psychological fact. He may require prolonged treatment to be freed from it; it is just as real as an actual cancer would have been. Not only do the illusions of individuals have psychological reality despite their objective falsity. The social, political and religious ideas which are held by most people in a society have a psychological reality, however false or one-sided they may be in point of objective fact. Indeed they form a psychic atmosphere which members of the society cannot help breathing.

(iii)

The secularist world view, which assumes that only the values of this world are real and important, is just such a psychological reality. The majority of Europeans and North Americans are profoundly influenced by it even when they profess to acknowledge a spiritual dimension. It is not so much a consciously held set of opinions as the spectacles through which people perceive the world of work and leisure,

14 Quoted Hostie, op. cit., p. 13

of family, of society and politics. Jung regarded this view as dangerously one-sided rather than wholly false. It was true in its affirmation of temporal and material values, false in its exaggeration of these to the point of ignoring or minimizing the equally real values of the spirit. He regarded modern secularism as the final stage of a centuries-long reaction against the one-sidedness of medieval Christendom which exalted spiritual values at the expense of the values of this world. Jung saw and described the beginnings of a revolution in the souls of Western men and women against secularism as decisive as the revolution which changed the direction of people's thinking at the end of the Middle Ages.

For medieval man the earth was the centre of the universe; the sun circled round it radiating its beneficent light and warmth. The motion of the stars in the night sky was caused by angelic beings who steered them on the courses marked out by divine providence. Over the whole cosmos God ruled; his hand painted the lily and cared for the sparrow; above all he had made men and women in his own image to be his sons and daughters. Heaven and hell were places whose geographical location was a matter of speculation but whose existence was unquestioned. Everyone knew what he must do to gain heaven and escape hell. The world was peopled with invisible spirits, both good and bad, who caused and cured illness, especially mental illness. Naturally not all the medievals accepted every detail of the medieval world view. The beginnings of modern experimental science were laid in the thirteenth century by men like the English friar, Roger Bacon, though in his case at the expense of being regarded as a heretic. Towards the end of the Middle Ages the atmosphere of the medieval world view came to be felt as oppressive by a growing number of intellectuals in the light of the knowledge of ancient Greek philosophy and science, which began to pour into Europe in the thirteenth century and after. The Renaissance came as a liberation to thousands of thoughtful people.

The founding fathers of modern science in the sixteenth and seventeenth centuries did not indeed reject the whole of the medieval world view. Nearly all of them took for granted the existence of God and his providence over the universe. It was not till later that complete agnosticism or atheism became common among the leading scientists and philosophers. Indeed it was the inner security that faith in God gave that enabled men to question all the received views of the natural world and to explore nature's mysteries with the tools of exact observation and experiment. It was the corporate, the taken-for-granted faith of the vast majority which conferred even on agnostics the confidence to make an absolute of so frail a plant as human reason. The apparent triumph of eighteenth-century rationalism, so Jung declared, had brought about its own nemesis. Despite the astonishing achievements of modern science and technology and the wealth and comfort of the affluent society of Europe and North America a growing number of persons today were disillusioned. They were hungry for the things of the spirit, for the spiritual food which the despised medieval Church gave to its members.

Jung explained this revolution in the soul of modern men and women with the help of an idea of the ancient Greek philosopher, Heracleitus, the idea expressed in the word *enantiodromia*, which means literally running into the opposite. The human soul is moved by opposite needs and instincts, the tension between which makes for vitality and creativity. But if one of these opposed tendencies is allowed free rein so as to exclude the other, then sooner or later a revulsion sets in to restore the balance and the situation is reversed. For example people in society want both order and freedom. In a healthy society these two opposed needs are held in creative tension. But if either is pressed too far, by a kind of pendulum swing it will bring about its opposite. To go all out in removing every restraint on individual freedom will in the end lead to the suppression of freedom under some form of dictatorship. For people will find the anarchy of unlimited freedom, in which everyone does what is right in his own eyes, so intolerable that they will be ready to welcome authoritarian government with enthusiasm. The medievals exalted the values of the spirit to the detriment of those of this world and the authority of divine revelation over that of human reason. In consequence, with the inevitability with which night succeeds day, a total reversal of values took place. During the centuries that followed the Middle Ages reason assumed a growing authority over against revelation, so that revelation came to be acceptable only in so far as it conformed to reason. This world and its values too became all-important and the things of the spirit of only secondary significance. The age of rationalism and secularism set in.

Jung noted and described many signs of a counter-revolution of the human spirit away from both secularism and rationalism. The evidence for this was first brought to Jung's notice by the patients who came to him from all over the world. A considerable number of these, all of them educated, were not suffering from any clinically definable neurosis; they were ill because they could find no meaning in life. Jung writes:

> I should like to call attention to the following facts. During the past thirty-five years people from all the civilized countries of the earth have consulted me. I have treated many hundreds of patients, the larger number being Protestants, a smaller number of Jews and not more than five or six believing Catholics. Among all my patients in the second half of life – that is over thirty-five – there has not been one whose problem in the last resort was not that of finding a religious outlook on life. It is safe to say that every one of them fell ill because he had lost what the living religions of every age give to their followers, and none of them has been really healed who did not regain his religious outlook. This has of course nothing whatever to do with a particular creed or membership of a church.[15]

Jung, as he makes clear, was speaking of individuals in middle life, most of them of assured position and in comfortable circumstances. The problems and neuroses of the young are usually different. We shall consider these later in connection with Jung's teaching about the stages of life.

The turn of the tide which Jung was noting fifty years ago is far more evident today than it was then. The secular attitude, concerned mainly with increasing the gross national product and raising the standard of living, is steadily losing its grip on men and women of the Western world. It is not

15 *C.W.*, vol. xi, para. 509

only the threat of Armageddon and planetary suicide or of mass starvation which is leading thoughtful people all over the world to question the direction in which civilization is moving. A powerful surge of the human spirit is seeking blindly to regain contact with the divine, and diffusing a mood of dissatisfaction with things as they are. One of the signs of the gathering revolution is the ennui, the boredom, present in the world today, which Teilhard de Chardin called public enemy number one. Among the negative signs of this movement of the human spirit are the widespread increase of violence, the reckless cult of sex, the mounting suicide rate, the attempt to escape down the blind alleys of drugs and alcohol and the other routes into fantasy and oblivion. Among the positive signs are the search for an alternative life-style, the commune movement, the growing interest in mysticism and the religions of the East.

One of the signs which Jung was noting well before the war was the growing interest in psychology. In the early 1930s Jung was writing:

> The rapid and world-wide growth of a psychological interest over the last two decades shows unmistakably that modern man has to some extent turned his attention from material things to his own subjective processes.[16]

He recognized this increasing interest in psychology to be by no means mainly due to scientific curiosity. Nor was the shocked fascination of the reading public at the writings of Freud and Havelock Ellis, with their disclosure of the large part played by sex in the background or the unconscious of respected and respectable citizens, due simply to prurience and the taste for the pornographic and the obscene. For the unconscious was not just a garbage heap for the morally unacceptable elements of human nature; it was also, so Jung was convinced, a source of life and creativity. The inner world of the unconscious exercised a magnetic attraction on minds starved of a genuine spiritual experience. Jung saw the interest in scientific psychology as only a tiny eddy in the great wave of curiosity concerning the occult and the irrational that was sweeping over the modern world. While theologians were labouring like their eighteenth-century predecessors to demonstrate the reasonableness of the Christian faith a growing public was taking an interest in astrology, spiritualism and black magic.

But if people were reacting against the dead greyness of scientific rationalism, they were not for the most part turning to the Christian Church. For the Church was felt to belong to the world of external reality from which they were turning away. There was a thirst for inner experience and a willingness to embrace any system or follow any leader that promised to lead them to it. Jung draws a parallel between movements flourishing in the early years of the twentieth century with second-century Gnosticism. He writes:

> The spiritual currents of the present have, in fact, a deep affinity with Gnosticism. . . . The modern movement which is most impressive numerically is undoubtedly theosophy, together with its continental sister, anthroposophy; these are pure Gnosticism in a Hindu dress. Compared with these movements the interest in scientific psychology is negligible. What is striking about gnostic systems is that they are based exclusively upon the manifestations of the unconscious, and that their moral teachings do not balk at the shadow side of life.[17]

Jung recognized in these movements much superstition and moral and intellectual perversity. But he saw that they would inevitably persist until they were replaced by something better. He saw them as embryonic stages from which in time new and riper forms would emerge. These exotic and sometimes bizarre systems were an attempt to satisfy deep religious needs and aspirations, which were not being met by Christian forms of worship. These were no longer felt to be meaningful. Because of the prestige of science these movements tended to be clothed in pseudo-scientific dress as spiritual or Christian science. These seekers were looking for a spiritual reality which could be experienced. They revolted against dogmatic

17 Ibid., para. 169

statements which had to be taken on faith and were not verifiable in experience.

I have dwelt on what Jung was describing half a century ago in order to call attention to the prophetic character of his writings. For the religious movements which seemed exotic in the years before the war are now a recognized part of the contemporary social scene. Schools of meditation of Hindu, Buddhist and Sufi inspiration have mushroomed and multiplied during the years since the war. Such movements as Transcendental Meditation, the Unification Church, the Children of Light, have all gained tens of thousands of adherents. The tide of eastern influence continues to flow and has perhaps not yet reached its zenith. The only effective response to this surge of the human spirit will come from those who will make the effort to understand the nature of the psychic energies at work.

The call of the unknown, which summoned generations of explorers to face the hazards and hardships of ocean, desert and forest, of tropical heat and Arctic ice and snow in order to survey and map the earth's surface, is now calling men and women to a new adventure: the exploration of the unknown inner world of the soul and the vast reaches of the unconscious. If we wish to take part in this new quest Jung is probably the wisest and most experienced guide available. He will show us how to dig down and clear out the rubble that clogs the ancient wells from which our ancestors drew the water of life. He will not ask us to reject the discoveries of modern science and the power it confers for good and ill. Rather he will show us how to draw from within ourselves the wisdom and strength needed to master and control the giant forces which science-based technology has placed at our disposal.

More importantly, I believe that Jung can help Christians to a deeper understanding of the life-renewing power of the gospel and the dynamism contained in ancient dogma. I think Jung's understanding of dogma to be partial and inadequate. He regarded dogma as a protection against a psychic experience which might otherwise have proved overwhelming, as an attempt to tame and domesticate dangerous psychic forces. No doubt this has been one of its functions. But perhaps because of his undervaluing of belief he failed fully to grasp the positive value of dogma. For Christian doctrine and dogma grew out of an attempt to define and map an intense spiritual experience; and dogma is one of the tools for the exploration of a reality which transcends human grasp. The creeds are not intended to be the final expression of ultimate truth but signposts pointing the way to unfathomable mystery. Christians who believe them to be accurate signposts need to take care not to identify the signposts with the realities to which they point. As under Jung's guidance we learn to get in touch with our own depths and discover our own truth, the powerful realities which the dogmas signify will become new and exciting. Further I believe that Jung can provide the ideas and language which will enable theologians and pastors to speak to the condition of their contemporaries and make the old gospel fresh and up to date.

Jung claimed that his ideas and theories were empirically based on observed psychic facts. As dreams, both his own and the many thousands submitted to him by his patients, were the principal source from which he gathered his evidence it will be necessary in the next chapter to plunge into this strange but fascinating underworld of the psyche.

2

DREAMS AND THEIR
INTERPRETATION

(i)

From time immemorial, men and women, old and young, have been deeply interested in their dreams. The Bible, both the Old Testament and the New, gives many accounts of dreams, which it was taken for granted were one of the ways in which God made known his will to men. Joseph, the youngest but one of the twelve sons of the patriarch Jacob, was both a dreamer and an interpreter of dreams. In his youth his dreams, which foretold his own eminence and the subjection of his parents and brothers to him, earned him an unpopularity which nearly proved fatal. Later, when a prisoner in Egypt, his ability to interpret Pharaoh's dreams about the fat and the lean cattle and the full and the withered ears of wheat led to his being appointed viceroy of Egypt. In the New Testament his namesake, Joseph, the husband of Mary, was twice warned in a dream by a messenger of God. Perhaps the most important dream recorded in the New Testament was Peter's dream on the roof-top at Joppa of a sheet descending from heaven upon which were many birds and beasts of a kind forbidden as food for Jews. A voice from heaven said, 'Rise, Peter, kill and eat.' To this Peter answered, 'Not so, Lord, I have never eaten anything unclean.' The voice replied, 'What God has cleansed you must not call unclean.'[1] This dream repeated three times marked an important turning point in the infant Church, cradled as it was in Judaism. For the dream together with certain events which followed convinced Peter that non-Jews could be admitted to membership in the Church. This prepared the way for the great influx of Gentiles into the young Christian movement and to its transformation from a Jewish sect into a universal Church.

In the early centuries of the Christian Church this biblical view of dreams as sometimes containing a message from God continued to be the accepted one. One of the most popular Christian writings of the second century was *The Shepherd of Hermas*, a work which contains many dreams and visions. The book was regarded by some as on a level with Scripture and, but for its disproportionate length, so it has been suggested, might even have been included as one of the books of the New Testament. However the willingness to treat dreams seriously gave way in the course of time to suspicion. It is possible to conjecture a number of reasons for this discrediting of dreams: the difficulty of interpreting dreams and the apparently trivial and inconsequential character of many dreams, the use of dreams by heretical sects to bolster up their beliefs, the suspect mental balance of some of those who claimed to interpret dreams, and, no doubt, the shift of interest to matters of seemingly greater and more practical importance. It was left to psychologists during the past hundred years to rehabilitate dreams in the western world as a valid source of knowledge.

The great pioneer in the exploration and interpretation of dreams in this recent period was Sigmund Freud, whose work and relationship to Jung was referred to in the last chapter. Freud regarded the dream as the royal road to the unconscious. Jung agreed with him wholeheartedly as to the importance of the dream as providing essential clues to the secrets of the unconscious but disagreed with him about their interpretation. Freud had discovered that much neurosis was caused by the frustration of the sex drive through the need to conform to the demands and expectations of parents and to

1   Acts 10:9–16

avoid shocking them. These repressed wishes express themselves in dreams by means of heavily disguised symbols which
the skilled interpreter could read. Jung, while agreeing that
dreams can shed light on the distant past and its traumas,
believed also that it offers the dreamer information about the
present state of the psyche and indeed about the future. Further he does not, like Freud, suppose that the difficulties of
interpretation are due to a kind of censorship exercised by the
unconscious, which deliberately disguises its meaning lest the
dreamer be shocked and wake up. Rather Jung affirms that
the dream presents in the symbolic language of dreams some
aspect of the present state of affairs in the unconscious. The
obscurity of the dream is due to our ignorance of its symbolic
language not to any intention of the unconscious to hide its
meaning. In exactly the same way a person ignorant of the
Chinese language or script would find it impossible to read
a Chinese book, not because the author was being intention-
ally obscure but because of his own ignorance. But the best
way to understand Jung's theories about dreams and their
interpretation is to consider some of the dreams which he
describes in his writings.

(ii)

In an essay on dreams[2] Jung describes how he was consulted
by a man who held a prominent place in the world. He was
troubled by feelings of anxiety and insecurity and complained
of dizziness and nausea, of a heavy head and difficulty in
breathing. Jung comments that this is an exact description of
mountain sickness. Of peasant parents he had made his way
up to his present relative eminence by ambition, industry and
talent. Step by step he had climbed to a position where further
opportunities of rising opened up before him. Then just at
this moment he was brought up suddenly by his neurosis.
Jung points out that his having all the symptoms of mountain
sickness was highly appropriate to the situation in which this
social climber found himself. He brought with him to the

2 *C.W.*, vol. xvi, paras 297–301

consultation two dreams of the previous night. The first dream was as follows:

> I am once more in the small village where I was born. Some peasant boys who went to school with me are standing in the street. I walk past them pretending not to know them. I hear one of them who is pointing at me say: 'He doesn't often come back to our village.'[3]

Jung comments that the interpretation of the dream is obvious; it is saying to the dreamer quite clearly: 'You forget how far down you began.' Here is the second dream:

> I am in a great hurry because I am going on a journey. I hunt up my baggage but cannot find it. Time flies and the train will soon be leaving. Finally I succeed in getting all my things together. I hurry along the street, discover I have forgotten a briefcase containing important papers, dash breathlessly back again, find it at last and then run towards the station, but make hardly any headway. With a final effort I rush on to the platform only to find the train steaming out into the yards. It is very long and runs in a curious S-shaped curve and will be thrown over by the speed of the train. As a matter of fact the driver opens the throttle as I try to shout. The rear coaches rock frightfully and are actually thrown off the rails. There is a terrible catastrophe. I awake in terror.[4]

The interpretation of this dream also is plain. The patient's struggle to pack up his things in time to catch the train pictures his intense anxiety to extend his social climb. The reckless engine-driver also depicts the patient's determination to press on at all costs. The crash indicates a neurosis which will effectively put an end to his social ambition. The patient has reached the summit of his career; the long ascent from his lowly origin has exhausted his strength. Instead of being content with his achievement he is driven by vaulting ambition to attempt heights for which he is not fitted. The neurosis came as a warning. Jung relates that circumstances

3   Ibid., para. 297
4   Ibid., para. 299

prevented him from treating the patient, who anyhow was not satisfied with his view of the case. The upshot was that events followed the course indicated in the dream. In trying to exploit his professional openings the patient ran so violently off the track that the train wreck was realized in actual life. The dream uttered a warning which he disregarded with fatal results.

Some dreams are prospective, pointing to the future. The seeds of the future are already present and at work in the unconscious; the possibilities of growth and decay are already within us and sometimes a dream may indicate them. Of course unforeseeable occurrences may falsify the dream predictions. Further the dreamer may change his attitude as a result of the dream and so bring its predictions to nothing. Had the patient paid heed to Jung's advice the dream would have been a warning of what might have happened rather than a prediction of what actually would take place. The warning dream resembles some of the Old Testament prophecies of judgement which were conditional. When Jonah proclaimed the imminent destruction of Nineveh on account of its wickedness the whole city, so the story runs, repented in sackcloth and ashes and changed its ways and was in consequence reprieved, much to the prophet's chagrin. Similarly the modern futurologist bases his forecasts on the assumption that present trends will continue and is thus frequently proved wildly wrong in a world where the new and the unpredictable are constantly occurring.

Jung gives an account of the prospective dream of a patient who came to him after having previously sought help unsuccessfully from two other doctors. The patient described the dream she had had the night before her first interview with Jung:

> I must cross a frontier or rather have already crossed it and find myself in a Swiss custom-house. I have only a handbag with me and believe that I have nothing to declare. But the customs official dives into my bag and to my astonishment pulls out two full-sized mattresses.[5]

5 Ibid., para. 310

Jung comments that the patient married during the course of her treatment with him but not without violent resistance to this step. 'My interpretation of the dream disappointed her greatly', writes Jung, 'but she was distinctly encouraged to go on in spite of all difficulties by the fact that the dream reported the frontier crossed already.'

The dream according to Jung has an important compensatory function. Indeed it is just one element in the compensatory mechanism of the unconscious. In this the psyche resembles its partner the body, which, as is well known, is an extremely complex self-regulating organism. Perhaps the best-known example of this is its in-built thermostatic system which in hot weather and cold maintains its temperature at a constant level, which in most individuals is 98.4°F. If our temperature varies only a degree or two from normal we begin to feel ill, which is part of the body's device to persuade us to take the steps necessary to put things right.

In a similar way the unconscious is at work pressing us to correct the one-sidedness or narrowness of our conscious aims and actions. Men and women are distinguished from their animal cousins by their power of concentrating on matters only remotely connected with biological necessity. In the pursuit of power or prestige we often do violence to fundamental needs of our nature. The unconscious is constantly seeking to modify and correct this high-handed attitude on the part of the conscious person towards his basic needs. A large part of the regulating process takes place during sleep in which the conscious mind lies passive and unresisting. While we are asleep the unconscious like an incoming tide sweeps away the mental sand-castles built during the day, leaving the sand smooth and clean and sometimes depositing on the beach strange objects from the deep sea in the shape of remembered dreams. Everyone has had the experience of going to bed worried and distressed and of waking up full of hope. Somehow during the night the unconscious has brought reassurance to the sleeper. Sometimes of course the opposite occurs. Perhaps without realizing it I have been refusing to face some disagreeable facts and have gone to bed confident and cheerful. Then in the morning I wake up vaguely troubled; my unconscious is warning me to think again. But the unconscious cannot carry out its work of rehabilitation and renewal without the co-operation of the conscious individual. The dream is one of the devices by means of which the unconscious seeks to bring home to an individual important facts which he has been overlooking. The dream of the train-wreck was an attempt by the unconscious to frighten the dreamer into changing his way of life; it was essentially compensatory.

The compensatory function of the unconscious provided Jung with one of the tools for elucidating the meaning of a dream. He would put to himself the question: 'What conscious attitude of the dreamer is the dream compensating for?' Here is the dream of a young man who consulted Jung:

> My father is driving away from the house in his new car. He drives very clumsily and I get very excited at his apparent stupidity. He goes this way and that, forward and backward, repeatedly getting his car into a tight place. He runs into a wall and badly damages the car. I shout at him in a perfect rage, telling him that he ought to behave himself. My father only laughs and then I see that he is dead drunk.[6]

The dream is completely at variance with the real-life situation. The young man is certain that his father would never behave like that even if he were drunk. The dreamer was himself used to cars, was a very careful driver and a very moderate drinker, especially before driving, and any injury to his car irritated him intensely. Further, his relationship with his father whom he admires for his success is excellent. Why should the unconscious paint his father in such unflattering colours, totally at variance with his actual character? Directly the question, what is the dream compensating for, is asked, the answer becomes plain. The young man is altogether too dependent on his father; his admiration for his father is preventing him from growing up and living his own life. The unconscious tries to correct this by depicting his father as a figure of fun. It depreciates the father in order to encourage the son to strike out a path on his own. Jung records that this

6 Ibid., para. 335

interpretation went home; the young man spontaneously acknowledged its truth.

The young man's acceptance of the interpretation of his dream illustrates another of Jung's principles of dream interpretation. No interpretation, he insists, can be accepted as certainly correct unless it wins the agreement of the dreamer himself. However sure a person may be of the correctness of his interpretation he must regard it as only a likely guess until it has won the assent of the dreamer. Even though an interpretation were in point of fact true, it would be of no use to the dreamer unless it rang bells for him. A purely intellectual understanding of a dream's meaning will be of small help to the dreamer towards changing his attitude in the manner the dream seems to indicate. For this he needs to *feel* the truth of it. This particular dream also well illustrates the highly coloured rhetorical devices of caricature, exaggeration and over-simplification that the unconscious employs to persuade the dreamer to take its message seriously.

A further means of elucidating the meaning of a dream, which Jung regarded as essential, is to ask the dreamer what the various dream symbols suggest to him. The amplifying of the meaning of the symbol by asking the dreamer to recall the associations of the symbol in his life and experience is an important preliminary to clarifying the sense of a dream. Unlike Freud who believed that each symbol had a fixed and determinate meaning, Jung believed that a symbol might have different meanings for different people. It is therefore important in seeking to interpret a dream to approach the task with an open mind, dismissing all preconceived notions, in order to listen to what the dream is actually saying.

(*iii*)

Some dreams, such as those already presented in this chapter, are relatively simple to interpret, given some knowledge of their context in the dreamer's life; dreams in which the symbols are drawn from the dreamer's personal experience. Other dreams however seem completely opaque and their symbols do not appear to have connections with anything in the dreamer's past life or his acquired knowledge. Such dreams need for their elucidation to be placed not merely in the context of the dreamer's past life and experience but in that of the human race. Jung calls the symbols in these dreams archetypal because they are universal, part of the inherited endowment of the human psyche. The means of amplifying and so establishing the meaning of these symbols are to be found in primitive religion and folklore, in mythology, fairy-tales and poetry.

Jung relates that he was once consulted about a seventeen-year-old girl. The clinical picture suggested organic disease but the girl showed hysterical symptoms as well. He asked about her dreams and she responded at once:

> Yes, I have terrible dreams. Just recently I dreamt that I was coming home at night. Everything is as quiet as death. The door into the living room is half open and I see my mother hanging from the chandelier and swinging to and fro in a cold wind that blows in from the open windows. At another time I dreamt that a terrible noise breaks out in the house at night. I go to see what has happened and find that a frightened horse is tearing through the rooms. At last it finds the door into the hall and jumps through the hall window from the fourth floor down into the street. I was terrified to see it lying below all mangled.[7]

Jung points out that the meaning of the dreams is to be found in two outstanding symbols, 'mother' and 'horse', which are clearly equivalent for they both commit suicide. To convey Jung's method of amplifying archetypal symbols I will quote in full what he says about these two symbols:

> The mother symbol is archetypal and refers to a place of origin, to nature, that which passively creates, hence to substance and matter, to material nature, the lower body and the vegetative functions. It also connotes the unconscious, natural and instinctive life, the physiological realm, the body in which we dwell and are contained; for the mother is also the vessel, the hollow form that carries and

7   Ibid., para. 343

nourishes, and it thus stands for the foundation of consciousness. Being within something or being contained in
something suggests darkness, the nocturnal, a state of
anxiety.[8]

With these allusions Jung proceeds:

> I am presenting the idea of the mother in many of its
> mythological and etymological transformations. All this is
> dream content but it is not something that the seventeen-
> year-old girl has acquired in her individual existence; it is
> rather a bequest from the past. On the one hand it has
> been kept alive by the language and on the other it is
> inherited with the structure of the psyche and is therefore
> to be found in all times and among all peoples. The familiar
> word 'mother' refers apparently to the best known of moth-
> ers, in particular to my mother. But the mother symbol
> points to a darker meaning which eludes conceptual for-
> mulation and can only be vaguely apprehended as the
> hidden nature-bound life of the body. Yet even this expres-
> sion is too narrow and excludes too many pertinent side-
> meanings. The psychic reality which underlies this symbol
> is so inconceivably complex that we can only discern it
> from afar off, and then but very dimly. It is such realities
> that call for symbolic expression. If we apply our under-
> standing to the dream its meaning will be: the unconscious
> life destroys itself. That is the dream's message to the
> dreamer and to every one who has ears to hear.[9]

After amplifying the meaning of the mother symbol Jung
proceeds to do the same for the horse archetype, which is
widely current in mythology and folklore.

> As an animal the horse represents the non-human psyche,
> the sub-human animal side and therefore the unconscious.
> This is why the horse in folklore sometimes sees visions,
> hears voices and speaks. As a beast of burden it is closely
> related to the mother archetype. The Valkyries carry the
> dead hero to Valhalla and the Trojan horse encloses the

8   Ibid., paras 344–5
9   Ibid., para. 346

Greeks. As an animal lower than man it represents the lower part of the body and the animal drives that take their rise from there. The horse is dynamic power and a means of locomotion; it carries one away like a surge of instinct. It is subject to panic like all instinctive creatures who lack higher consciousness. Also it has to do with sorcery and magical spells – especially the black night horse which is the herald of death.[10]

Jung goes on:

It is evident that the horse is the equivalent of the mother with a slight shift of meaning. The mother stands for life at its origin, the horse for the merely animal life of the body. If we apply this meaning to the dream it says: the animal life destroys itself. The two dreams make nearly the same assertion but, as is usually the case, the second is more specific. The peculiar subtlety of the dream is brought out in both instances: there is no mention of the death of the individual. It is notorious that one often dreams of one's own death, but that is no serious matter. When it is really a question of death the dream speaks another language. Both of these dreams point to a serious and even fatal organic disease. The prognosis was shortly after borne out in fact.[11]

I have given Jung's interpretation of these two dreams in his own words in order to illustrate the thoroughness with which he uses mythology and folklore to draw out the meaning of the archetypal symbols. If some of the material seems far-fetched or irrelevant to the interpretation of the dreams, it all helps to build up a sense of the depth, complexity and sheer mystery of the psychic reality which finds expression in them. The individual who often feels his life to be insignificant is hedged about by vast, unknown realities which speak to him in his sleep.

The two dreams make a good introduction to Jung's theories about archetypes and the collective unconscious. Over and above the personal unconscious which contains the

10 Ibid., para 347
11 Ibid., 349

forgotten experiences of an individual's life from infancy onwards, there is a deeper layer of inherited racial experience
which is handed on to each individual at birth in the form of
archetypes. Archetype is the name Jung gives to certain inherited tendencies of the psyche closely allied to instinct.
Indeed they might almost be called the cognitive factor in
instinct, the eye by which instinct perceives the object that
will satisfy it, or a kind of instinctive knowledge. This knowledge is transmitted not in the form of abstract ideas but of
images, or rather of an instinctive tendency to respond to
certain images. Thus the image of the mother's breast triggers
off in the infant his inborn knowledge of the breast as a source
of food. We can see something corresponding to Jung's archetypes at work in the sub-human animal kingdom. The
spawning of salmon, the nest-making instinct of the thrush,
the migratory urge of the swallow, the extraordinarily complex behaviour of ants, wasps and other insects, are evidence
of a similar inborn tendency to respond to certain stimuli, in
other words to archetypes.

In the course of thousands of years mankind has been
confronted many times over with certain typical situations
and has developed certain ways of dealing with them. This
racial wisdom is embodied in the myths and stories which all
races possess as well as in the formation of language. Jung
preserved an open mind as to how far this racial experience
was transmitted genetically and how far through a kind of
participation mystique in the collective unconscious of the human
race. It is clear that in some way or other this transmission
does take place. I quote from a theologian:

> The human imagination has always been controlled by
> certain basic images, in which man's own nature, his re-
> lation to his fellows, and his dependence on the divine
> power find expression. The individual did not make them
> for himself. He absorbs them from the society in which he
> is born, partly through the suggestion of outward acts and
> the significance of words, partly, it would seem, by some
> more hidden means of appropriation. The contents of other
> people's minds flow into ours at a subconscious level, a fact
> constantly evidenced and as constantly disbelieved. The

ancestral images of which we speak may, it would seem, be carried to the next generation by those who are unaware of their existence at the conscious level.[12]

So, in addition to dream symbols whose interpretation requires the dreamer's conscious associations there are archetypal symbols which need some knowledge of mythology, folklore and the etymology of language for their elucidation. The archetypal symbols which occurred in the dreams just discussed are two out of a great many. Such symbols can make us aware of the evolutionary stages through which the human psyche has passed. Dreams contain images and express instincts which belong to the most primitive levels of human nature.

There are many levels of the psyche and many degrees of unconsciousness. In his autobiography Jung describes a remarkable dream of his own which illustrates his theories about the structure of the psyche and perhaps helped him to formulate them:

> I was in a house I did not know which had two storeys. It was 'my' house. I found myself in the upper storey where there was a kind of salon furnished with fine old pieces in rococo style. On the walls hung a number of precious old paintings. I wondered that this should be my house and thought 'not bad'. But then it occurred to me that I did not know what the lower floor looked like. Descending the stairs I reached the ground floor. There everything was much older, and I realized that this part of the house must date from about the fifteenth or sixteenth century. The furnishings were medieval, the floors were of red brick. Everywhere it was rather dark. I went from one room to another thinking 'now I really must· explore the whole house'. I came upon a heavy door and opened it. Beyond it I discovered a stone stairway that led down into the cellar. Descending again I found myself in a beautiful vaulted room which looked exceedingly ancient. Examining the walls I discovered layers of brick among the ordinary stone blocks and chips of brick in the mortar. As soon as

12 Farrer, *Rebirth of Images* (Dacre Press 1948), p. 13

I saw this I knew that the walls dated from Roman times.
My interest by now was intense. I looked more closely at
the floor. It was of stone slabs and in one of these I discovered a ring. When I pulled it the stone slab lifted and
again I saw a staircase of narrow stone steps leading into
the depths. These too I descended and entered a low cave
cut into the rock. Thick dust lay on the floor, and in the
dust were scattered bones and broken bits of pottery, like
the remains of a primitive culture. I discovered two human
skulls, obviously very old and half disintegrated. Then I
awoke.[13]

Jung comments:

It was plain to me that the house represented a kind of
image of the psyche – that is of my then state of consciousness with hitherto unconscious additions. Consciousness
was represented by the salon. It had an inhabited atmosphere in spite of its antequated style. The ground floor
stood for the first level of the unconscious. The deeper I
went the more alien and the darker the scene became. In
the cave I discovered the remains of a primitive culture,
that is the world of the primitive man within myself – a
world that can scarcely be reached or illumined by consciousness. The primitive psyche of man borders on the life
of the animal soul, just as the caves of pre-historic times
were usually inhabited by animals before man laid claim
to them.[14]

The dream well illustrates the depths and the many levels of
the psyche. For Jung the important distinction is between the
personal unconscious, the level nearest to consciousness, and
the various levels of the collective unconscious. The personal
unconscious contains the forgotten or repressed memories of
an individual's personal life. The more he is able to accept
these memories and tendencies as his own possession the
more his personality will gain in strength and inner coherence.
But the collective unconscious is another matter. The contents

13 *Memories, Dreams and Reflections*, pp. 182–3
14 Ibid., p. 184

of this level of the psyche are not his personal possession but the shared possession of mankind. Archetypal forces are at work in it from which he can derive energy and wisdom; but if he tries to identify with them and possess them he will become their victim. So far from his possessing and dominating them, they will dominate him, dwarfing his human characteristics and destroying his individual identity. A man who has attained to a position of authority may derive inner strength and wisdom from the king archetype, the principle of rulership, but only if he refuses to identify with it. He needs the humility and strength to keep constantly aware of his own ordinary humanity and to see himself as the steward and guardian of a power and wisdom for rulership which is not his own personal possession. It is the possession of the human race and is something to be exercised for the common good. The twentieth century affords many examples of men who have been possessed by this archetype and through it have unleashed demonic forces which have not only maimed their own humanity but have inflicted barbarous cruelties on their fellows.

(iv)

An important part of Jung's therapeutic method consists in encouraging the individual to allow the unconscious, partly through the influence of dreams, to modify the mistakes or one-sidedness of his conscious attitude. For this reason it is necessary to stress his insistence that the individual must hold firmly to the real values of his conscious personality. If the conscious personality is destroyed or even crippled there is no one left to assimilate what the unconscious presents. Jung writes:

> We must see to it that the conscious personality remains intact, for we can only turn the unconscious compensations to good account when the conscious personality co-operates in the venture.[15]

15 I have been unable to trace this quotation

The powerful drives and volcanic energies which we inherit from a long line of ancestors can be likened to a broad and swift-flowing river. Each individual needs to learn how to paddle his own personal canoe on the hurrying waters and to avoid being capsized or carried away by the current. To do this he needs to have confronted and learnt from his own personal experiences and to know something of his own strengths and weaknesses. No one manages this task set by life perfectly. In extreme cases of failure there may be complete mental breakdown. I may be convinced that I am Solomon or Julius Caesar or even Jesus Christ. Fantasy may become more real to me than daily life and I may have to be taken care of. Many of the patients in mental homes are living in a nightmare. Everything that happens around them is interpreted in the light of their fantasies which are more real to them than the people and surroundings of their day-to-day lives. They have been carried away by the river and lost control of their canoe. It is therefore of first importance for the individual to realize his distinctness from the underground fires and explosive energies, and the archetypal images through which they can bewitch the mind.

The great controlling power which has on the whole prevented the primeval urges of mankind from breaking out destructively is religion. For the symbols and truth-embodying stories or myths of religion give meaning to the deepest human longings and so enable mankind to live in relative peace. The waning power of Christianity as a dominant influence in the West during the last few centuries has left Europeans feeling lost and insecure and therefore vulnerable to destructive forces from within. The most obvious example is the upsurge of demonic paganism in Nazi Germany which led to the most destructive of all wars and the barbarous holocaust of six million Jews. But it is also evident in the outbreaks of violence all over the world today. In his autobiography Jung recalls a recurrent dream which during the years 1913 and 1914 spoke of the violence about to break out. He used to dream during the months preceding the war of rivers of blood flowing over Europe. Sometimes the dream even broke into his consciousness in the daytime in the form of a waking vision. Not till war broke out in August 1914 did he understand the dream's meaning. It was a prophetic message from the unconscious of the collective violence and bloodshed that was about to take place.

One further example will help to illustrate Jung's method of interpreting dreams.

A man once came to me for a first consultation. He told me that he was engaged in all sorts of learned pursuits and was also interested in psycho-analysis from a literary point of view. He was in the best of health, he said, and was not to be considered in any sense a patient. He was merely pursuing his psycho-analytical interests. He was very comfortably off and had plenty of time to devote himself to his pursuits. He wanted to make my acquaintance in order to be inducted by me into the theoretical secrets of analysis. He admitted that it must be very boring for me to have to do with a normal person, since I must find mad people much more interesting. He had written to me a few days before to ask when I could see him. In the course of conversation we soon came to the question of dreams. I thereupon asked him if he had had a dream the night before he visited me. He affirmed this and told the following dream: *I was in a bare room. A sort of nurse received me, and wanted me to sit at a table on which stood a bottle of fermented milk which I was supposed to drink. I wanted to go to Dr Jung, but the nurse told me that I was in hospital and that Dr Jung had no time to receive me.* It is clear even from the manifest content of the dream that the anticipated visit to me had somehow constellated the unconscious. He gave the following associations: *Bare room*: a sort of frosty reception room, in an official building or the waiting room of a hospital. I was never in a hospital as a patient. *Nurse*: she looked repulsive, she was cross-eyed. That reminds me of a fortune-teller and palmist whom I once visited to have my fortune told. Once I was sick and had a deaconess as a nurse. *Bottle of fermented milk*: Fermented milk is nauseating, I cannot drink it. My wife is always drinking it, and I make fun of her for this because she is obsessed with the idea that one must always be doing something for one's health. I remember that I was once in a sanatorium – my nerves were not so good – and there I had to drink fermented milk.

At this point I interrupted him with the indiscreet question: had his neurosis entirely disappeared since then? He tried to worm out of it, but finally had to admit that he still had his neurosis, and that actually his wife had for a long time been urging him to consult me. But he certainly did not feel so nervous that he had to consult me on that account, he was after all not mad, and I treated only mad people. It was only that he was interested in learning about my psychological theories, etc.

Jung continues:

From this we can see how the patient has falsified the situation. It suits his fancy to come to me in the guise of a philosopher and psychologist and to allow the fact of his neurosis to recede into the background. But the dream reminds him of it in a very disagreeable way and forces him to tell the truth. He has to swallow this bitter drink. His recollection of the fortune-teller shows us very clearly just how he had imagined my activities. As the dream informs him he must first submit to treatment before he can get to me.[16]

As Jung comments, the dream rectifies the situation by contributing the material that was lacking and thereby improving the patient's attitude. The dream illustrates Jung's method of amplifying the significant dream images, the bare room, the fermented milk, the nurse, with the help of the dreamer's associations. Only then does the message of the dream become clear. The dream further illustrates the compensatory function of the unconscious which seeks to undermine the self-confidence of the dreamer by painting a vivid picture of his true condition.

I have dwelt at length on Jung's theories about dreams and their interpretation partly because they provide a large part of the empirical evidence upon which his psychology is based. For many years he was in the habit of analysing from fifteen

16 *C.W.*, vol. viii, paras 478–82

hundred to two thousand dreams a year. It was only after he had considered and analysed many thousands of dreams that he ventured to publish his hypotheses based upon them. Jung constantly affirmed that in dealing with the unconscious we are confronting a highly mysterious reality. Dreams are the royal road into this largely unknown region and his theories about them, which he always recognized to be incomplete, are a valuable companion for those who would travel the road and explore the region. Further the dream is a phenomenon which both the Bible and the early Church took seriously as one of the modes by which God made known his will. A careful attention to dreams can help the Christian believer to a fuller realization of God's guiding hand in his life. It can help to make the idea of God's providence real.

3

GOD'S PROVIDENCE AND THE SELF

(i)

The consideration of dreams in the previous chapter introduced us to a number of ideas central to Jung's psychology, some of which we shall have to explore more thoroughly later. Among these ideas was that of the archetypes, which Jung understood to be inborn tendencies within the psyche, closely linked with instinct, which predispose us to respond to certain images and themes. There are many of these inherited tendencies and in this chapter I shall consider one of them, the archetype of the self. Jung regarded this archetype as in some respects the most important of them all and it is fundamental to his understanding of religion.

This book is in part my personal attempt to articulate the way in which Jung's ideas have helped me to a fuller realization of the Christian faith. The truth that Jung has especially brought home to me is that of God's providence over human life and of my own life in particular. It is therefore necessary to outline briefly what belief in God's providence means. The doctrine is no peripheral one but is central to the belief that God is the creator and sustainer of all that is. It affirms that within and around every item of the universe from the largest of the giant stars to the tiniest sub-atomic particle there lives an infinite fountain of active benevolence and an inexhaustible fund of invention and contrivance. The doctrine is understood by contemporary theologians in such a manner as to support the regularities that the natural scientist observes and measures. As Austin Farrer has written:

> God makes the world make itself; or rather, since the world is not a single being, he makes the multitude of created forces make the world, in the process of making or being themselves. It is this principle of divine action that gives the world such endless vitality, such vital variety in every part. The price of it is that the agents God employs in the basic levels of the structure will do what they will do, whether human convenience is served by it or not. Yet the creative persuasion has brought it about that there is a world, not a chaos, and that in this world there are men.[1]

The doctrine of divine providence, or creative persuasion as Farrer calls it, is an essential part of the Christian idea of God; for either God must be in everything or he is in nothing. This I accepted as true before ever I became interested in Jung. It was part of what I meant by God. But being a man of the twentieth century I was also concerned to have some awareness of God, some experience of God to support my faith; and it was here that Jung helped. Though God, as I believe, is present in everything that happens he is not experienced equally strongly in everything. Jung helped me to identify the action of God in part of my experience and so strengthened my faith in his presence everywhere. In particular Jung's teaching about the self provided the link between my theoretical belief in God's providence and my recognition of it in my day-to-day living.

Jung derived the term 'self' from Indian religious thought but gave it a meaning of his own. By the self he referred to the total personality, both the conscious, reflecting, planning element in the personality, which he termed the ego, and the unconscious, in which he included both the personal and the collective unconscious, both the forgotten memories of past experience and the inherited archetypal tendencies which we share with the rest of the human race. The self is a dynamic concept which Jung invented to describe an immensely

1   Farrer, *The Science of God* (Bles 1966), pp. 90–1

powerful psychic reality which was apprehended in two different but closely related ways. This reality was experienced first as a pressure upon the conscious individual of a whole of which he was a small but important part. It was also experienced as a centre of magnetic attraction within the personality. Jung uses the term 'self' to include both these felt realities, the total personality and the personality centre.

He was led to formulate the theory partly by reflecting on an eastern symbol, the mandala. This symbol, usually in the form of a circle or square, often intricately patterned and having a centre, was designed as a focus for meditation. The mandala symbol occurred frequently in Jung's own dreams and in those of his patients. He regarded it as a symbol of the self, of the total personality, and so of wholeness. Further in dreams it often carried a strong sense of the numinous; it was both awe-inspiring and fascinating and carried an immense authority. Jung appears to find it hard to distinguish the experience of the self and that of God.

The influence of the self, of the largely unknown whole of which the conscious person is but a part, is all-pervasive, though seldom recognized for what it is. Sometimes it acts upon us like the swing of a pendulum, pulling us first one way and then another, from an urge to action to a need to be passive, to be acted upon; from the need to go out to others to the equally pressing need to retire into ourselves. Sometimes, under the influence of majestic scenery or haunting music, the magic of great art or the atmosphere of a solemn religious rite, it is felt like the breaking in of a new world. Sometimes under the stress of perplexity or the weight of some heavy responsibility or sorrow it is felt like an influx of wisdom and power guiding, fortifying and holding us secure. Sometimes, as in the case of Socrates, it is felt as an authoritative voice, warning us against some action that we have been contemplating. Sometimes when we have acted contrary to what we know at a deep level to be right it is felt as a judge reproving us.

It was Jung's idea of the self, the whole personality, acting as a constant influence on my conscious aims and intentions in a manner which I was powerless to prevent, that brought home to me the inescapable reality of God's rule over my life.

So long as I thought of God's providence as an abstract truth, part of theistic belief, it made no powerful impact upon me. But it was quite another matter if God's guiding hand was within my own being, within the fluctuations of mood and the ups and downs of health. As an individual endowed with free will I was free to go my own way regardless of what God's will might be, but I could in no way prevent the repercussions within myself which were the direct and immediate consequence of my disregarding God. I came to understand that to resist God was to run counter to the law of my own being; God's judgement worked through a kind of in-built psychic mechanism; it was self-acting and imposed from within me. My punishment in the shape of unwelcome feelings of guilt, anxiety or depression was self-inflicted. To say that God can be experienced within the working of the human psyche does not, of course, imply he is not present and perceptible outside it. To quote Farrer again:

> The action of God must be taken to be universal. But when we claim this we cannot be expected to claim that God's active presence comes home to us with equal clarity at every point in the universe. There is more theology to be dug out of a saint than out of a sandpit.[2]

In a strikingly realistic way Jung has brought to light the old truth that God who is present everywhere is most accessible to us within our own souls.

Those who profess no religious faith do not, most of them, actively disbelieve in God; they merely fail to see the relevance of faith to the tasks and problems of living. They experience the influence of the self and its disconcerting effects in their lives without in any way connecting it with God. If they can be shown that this experience is closely related to the God whom believers worship, the question of faith and religious practice would suddenly become important to them. Some believers on the other hand are likely to be surprised and even put out to be told that the God, whom they approach at a discreet distance through the liturgy of the Church, was a powerful and disturbing presence in their everyday life. Yet

2 Ibid., p. 17

others may feel that the endeavour of psychology to look into and try to understand the experience of God is an attempt to tear away the veil from a relationship which ought to be kept secret. There is of course much in the soul's relationship to God which will always be mysterious, for we have no means of measuring the divine. But there is a human element in this relationship which it is right to attempt to understand. A living faith is always in search of fuller understanding; it is a lamp which sheds light on what without it would be dark and obscure.

The pressure of the self upon our conscious aims and intentions is most readily felt when it appears to be working against us, just as a swimmer becomes aware of the strength of a current when he is swimming against it. So it may well be that an individual's first experience of God is of his judgement. God's judgement is however always merciful and is in fact persuading him to change the attitude which is causing inner division and frustration. It is his refusal to follow the guidance of the self that causes his inner frustration. The unwillingness to change, the resistance to the self's pressure is a frequent cause of neurosis.

It is often thought that that an intellectual understanding of the psychological causes of a neurosis will of itself effect a cure. But it will not do this unless the insight leads to a change of attitude. Jung describes the case of a highly intelligent young man who came to him for help. He had worked out a detailed analysis of his neurosis after a serious study of medical literature.

He brought me his findings in the form of a precise and well-written monograph fit for publication, and asked me to read the manuscript and tell him why he was not cured. He should have been according to the verdict of science as he understood it. After reading his manuscript I was forced to grant that, if it were only a question of insight into the causal connections of a neurosis, he should in all truth have been cured. Since he was not, I supposed that this must be due to the fact that his attitude to life was somehow fundamentally wrong – though I had to admit that his symptoms did not betray it. In reading his account of his life I had noticed that he often spent his winters at St Moritz or Nice. I therefore asked him who paid for these holidays, and it thereupon came out that a poor school teacher who loved him had cruelly deprived herself in order to indulge the young man in these visits to pleasure-resorts. His want of conscience was the cause of his neurosis, and it is not hard to see why scientific understanding failed to help him. His fundamental error lay in his moral attitude. He found my way of looking at it shockingly unscientific, for morals have nothing to do with science. He supposed that by invoking scientific thought he could spirit away the immorality which he himself could not stomach. He would not even admit that the conflict existed because his mistress gave him the money of her own free will.[3]

To this account we may add the comment that the young man's lack of concern for the woman who loved him did violence to elements in himself which in most people would have caused a painful sense of guilt. But his scientific notions kept all sense of wrong-doing repressed. Something deeper in him than his conscious personality brings pressure upon him to persuade him to repent. The neurotic symptoms were a substitute for the sense of guilt which might have led him to change his attitude and behaviour.

(ii)

The inescapable pressure of the total personality upon the conscious individual is one of the ways by which God's judgement is made effective in the lives of men and women. But the same pressure when recognized and responded to positively becomes the means of healing and renewal. Directly I change my attitude and admit my fault or my folly, not merely verbally but with a real inward alteration of feeling expressed in outward behaviour, then at once the healing waters begin to flow as from some deep spring within myself; the parched desert begins to blossom and I am inundated with a sense of peace. Just as God's judgement is brought about partly through the law inscribed on the human heart, which automatically works against those who transgress it, so similarly the renewing grace of God begins to heal and liberate those who turn and submit to this inner law. St John's Gospel records words of Jesus which exactly describe this experience: 'He that believeth in me . . . out of his belly shall flow rivers of living water.'[4] The evangelist comments that this living water is none other than the Spirit of God. Further this life-renewing Spirit flows from the belly, the symbol of a centre within us which is also the seat of powerful emotion.

The belief that God guides us from the centre of our being can completely transform the idea of obedience to God's will. The duty of obeying God has often been conceived of as though it meant submitting to an authority external to us and over against us. Many have revolted against such an obedience because it seemed to belittle their dignity and proper independence. But if the authority to which I have to submit is within me, then the more I conform myself to its directions the more at one I shall be in myself and the more inner-directed. The more completely and spontaneously I follow the directions of this inner guide the more truly I shall be myself, the more I shall be able to realize and live out my own individual truth. In the phrase of a well-known prayer God's service is perfect freedom. So far from diminishing my dignity and proper independence as a human being this obedience enhances it.

This Jungian-inspired interpretation of God's providential rule, according to which God is understood to identify himself with me as in a manner the soul of my soul and the centre of my being – as indeed he must be of every man and woman – is powerful and liberating. It can, I believe, help to make the idea of God real and important to many questioning men and women today. We must now turn to consider whether Jung's ideas can throw light on the distinctively Christian faith in Jesus Christ. Christians claim that salvation, complete wholeness, comes through Jesus Christ and through him alone. This claim has been understood in a narrowly exclusive

4 John 7:38

way that would shut out the majority of the human race from salvation; but this is not the only way in which Christians understand it. St John's Gospel declares that God's Word became man in the flesh and blood of Jesus Christ, that God spoke to man through the medium of that human life. But before that immense affirmation was made the Gospel had declared that the Word is the light of all men everywhere. All men at least potentially have a capacity to respond to the divine. The intimations of the divine, of which some people are strongly aware and others hardly at all, are received partly through the religious traditions in which individuals grow up, partly through the light of the divine Word shining in the human mind and heart. If we follow Jung we should understand the Word influencing the individual men and women through the pressure of the self upon their conscious personalities. In all the religious traditions and cultures ignorance and errors mingle with truth. Further there are all sorts of hindrances, social, moral and psychological, which prevent a person from recognizing and responding wholeheartedly to God's voice. Nevertheless the Christian must believe that all that is true and valuable in the ethical and religious ideas that guide the lives of men and women are derived from the light of the Word. There had been a long preparation for the coming of the Word in the man, Jesus of Nazareth. In the words of Irenaeus, a bishop in Gaul at the end of the second century, the Word was accustoming himself to mankind and mankind to himself. Irenaeus had in mind the preparation of Israel for the new entrance of the Word into human life. But everywhere and at all times the Word has been secretly at work educating men and women so that they might recognize and respond to him. Part of the purpose of the life of Christ, his teaching, his death, his rising again and his continuing presence through the Holy Spirit in the Christian community, is to correct, interpret and crown all the half-lights, the partly perceived truths, the one-sided insights, the whisperings of the divine Word in the diverse religious traditions and in the hidden depths of the human heart.

Jung's theory of the self, as I understand it, sheds light on the way in which the Word does actually renew the lives of men and women. In Jesus of Nazareth we have a picture in the vivid colours of a particular human life of the character of the divine pressure which is all the time at work upon us. Jesus Christ presents us with a clue to the nature of the powerful inner force which is ceaselessly urging us to change, to make the decisions and do the deeds which will enable us to grow to our full stature as human beings, to become what we truly are, to realize our own truth.

The Christian's assurance that in Jesus Christ he has to do with a presence and power active within him is much needed. For the transformation which the individual must undergo if he is to fulfil his destiny and live out his own truth demands courage and the will to persevere. His growth cannot be automatic like the growth of an oak out of the acorn in which its vitality was once contained. Each individual must co-operate with the power working in him by a certain trust and by decisions whose outcome is beyond his horizon. There is an inertia, a resistance to change which has to be overcome and there is an instinctive fear of arousing the volcanic energies asleep within, lest they prove uncontrollable. Nevertheless if we are to grow to our full human height these dangerous energies must be faced; we must be ready to say goodbye to the familiar and the safe in order to allow a new and strange-seeming attitude to be born and grow. The believer who can see the forces of change at work in him as the summons of the same God who disclosed himself in the man of Nazareth is strengthened and reassured. He can understand the pressures as the voice of Christ saying, 'Follow me' and 'Fear not, only believe'. His reliance on Christ will foster the courage and steadfastness he needs to fulfil his destiny.

Jung gives the name individuation to the process of development marked by crises by which an individual learns step by step to accept and live out what he truly is. More will be said later about the individuation process. Here it must suffice to say that it is a natural movement of growth which will reach fulfilment unless it is frustrated by the fears of the individual. For he needs to face and come to terms with elements of his being which may fill him with terror or disgust. From our infancy onwards we are subjected to strong pressure from society – from parents, schoolteachers and other important figures in our lives – to conform to what people expect of us. This is necessary and unavoidable if we are to grow up civilized. But the mental attitudes and habits, which we form in our efforts to adapt to society, and the fear of criticism or ridicule if we fail to conform cause us to repress much of the instinctive urges and impulses of our nature; and these elements of ourselves in their repressed condition take on a sinister aspect. The inner energies which we feel at work within us seem not only dangerous but evil. It takes courage to risk confronting them; but only through this confrontation can a person discover his own individual path. For the process of individuation requires a person to face and enter into a creative relationship with his unconscious energies and instinctive drives. This is an arduous task imposed by life which analysis is designed to assist. When an individual undergoes analysis the presence of the analyst and the mutual relationship of patient and analyst are an integral part of the analytical procedure. The patient comes to rely on the analyst whose personality reassures him and enables him to let go of the fears which are blocking the movement of healthy growth. The Christian's trust in Christ is in some ways analogous to the patient's reliance on his analyst. For faith in Christ enables the believer similarly to surrender the fears which are inhibiting his growth to freedom. There is of course the great difference that the analyst is visibly present to his patient while the presence of Christ is invisible and can only be recognized by faith. Nevertheless the unseen presence of Christ is mediated and made real to the believer by things which are seen. Through the pages of the New Testament, pondered with faith and imagination, Christ's presence, challenging and reassuring, can be made vivid to the believer. Further, association with his fellow believers in worship, sacrament and friendship can equally make real the invisible Christ who is the Head of his Body, the Church.

(iii)

Jung's psychology is both a set of theories and a praxis, a system of psychotherapy. Indeed theory and practice are closely interrelated; his theories, empirically based, are framed to account for the psychic facts uncovered in his psychological work. In this it resembles Christianity which is both a set of beliefs and a way of life that are mutually interdependent. Christian theology has grown out of the endeavour to understand and explain the new life, the wholeness and freedom, which men and women found and find through their faith in Jesus Christ. The New Testament is plainly the work of men whose lives have been changed by their faith in Christ. Whenever Christian belief has come to be felt as a set of truths only remotely connected with experience then Christianity has grown feeble. It was this enfeebled Christianity against which Jung strongly reacted in his youth. There are many signs today of a hunger among Christians for an experience of the truths believed in, of which the best known is the charismatic or pentecostalist revival. I believe that in a style very different from modern pentecostalism Jung's psychology can help Christians to recover a sense of the reality of God, of Christ and of the new life through him.

Jung's concept of the self, as he was well aware, accords closely with the Christian mystical tradition, especially as we meet it in the fourteenth and the two following centuries. The theology which provided the intellectual basis for this tradition assumed the immanence of the transcendent God throughout the universe and therefore within the human soul. But the tradition was also founded on experience, for the mystical quest is the search for an experienced union with God. The spiritual guides who stand in this tradition teach that God who is present everywhere is most surely to be found within the individual's own soul; it is here that he is most accessible. They make use of a number of metaphors to help a person to focus his attention on the divine mystery within. Sometimes God is spoken of as dwelling in the apex, the high point of the soul, which suggests perhaps that the knowledge of God transcends all other knowledge. Sometimes God is understood as dwelling in the *fundus*, the base, of the soul. This image suggests that God is to be found in the lowest depths of the soul, that the soul is grounded in God and that the experience of God is the most fundamental of all experiences. But perhaps the commonest symbolic locus of the divine presence is that of the soul's centre. We find this symbol used by the fourteenth-century Julian of Norwich and the sixteenth-century St Teresa and St John of the Cross, to quote well known names. The three ways of symbolizing the divine presence in the soul – in the summit, the base and the centre – taken together build up a conception not unlike Jung's idea of the self, the total personality, whose influence upon the individual is the means by which he becomes aware of God. For the pressure of the self is experienced not only as a vast encompassing reality but as a magnetic point of attraction, a jewel, in the personality centre.

In *The Interior Castle* St Teresa represents the soul as a great house containing many rooms. She describes the spiritual journey as a progress in which the individual is led by stages closer and closer to the central room where God dwells. It would be over-simple to identify the journey towards union with God with the individuation process, but it looks as though the two movements must be related. The God of grace who draws the individual to seek and find him is the author of all natural processes and therefore of the individuation process. Grace perfects and neither destroys nor bypasses nature though it transcends it. Some understanding of the individuation process should greatly help the Christian in his spiritual quest.

A problem which many moderns find if they approach the writings of the old mystics is that their teachings date from a pre-critical period, weak in its ability to distinguish between fact and fancy. We tend to view this period through a romantic haze as a time when knights jousted or rode out seeking adventure and all sorts of marvels were credible. The age seems far removed from the science and science-based technology of the twentieth century with its television and jet-travel, its computers and electronically programmed robots. But when a psychologist of our own day, as a result of the painstaking investigation of the experience of many hundreds of individuals, is forced by the facts to frame hypotheses which closely resemble the teaching of the old spiritual guides, we are compelled to take notice. For in the writings of Jung we see much of the old teaching transposed into the idiom of twentieth-century psychology. Expressed in the language of faith and devotion congenial to those earlier times the teaching is apt to seem unreal, but translated into the idiom of dynamic psychology this seemingly out-of-date teaching becomes grippingly real and relevant.

Not only does Jung's account of the structure of the psyche accord well with the old tradition but his therapeutic method follows a not dissimilar path. One of the basic principles of Jung's method is to encourage the patient to become aware of what is going on below the level of his conscious thinking and planning. He encourages him, for example, to pay serious attention to his dreams, to his waking fantasies and day-dreams and to the thoughts and impulses which rise unbidden into consciousness. Instead of ignoring these visitors who knock and enter the conscious mind, the patient is encouraged to look at them, to try to understand them and the unconscious wishes that they voice, so as to become more aware of himself in depth. This closely resembles the injunctions of the old spiritual guides to dwell in the cell of self-knowledge, to direct the attention constantly to the hidden motives which underlie our conscious aims and actions. The author of the anonymous fourteenth-century treatise on mystical prayer, *The Cloud of Unknowing*, bids the reader:

> Swink and sweat in all that thou can'st and mayest for to get thee a true knowing and feeling of thyself as thou art. And then I trow soon after that thou wilt get thee a true knowing and feeling of God as he is.[5]

The passage is referring not to a merely intellectual or theoretical knowledge of human nature but to a real self-awareness such as the modern psychotherapist seeks to elicit. Further we see in this six-centuries-old treatise an anticipation of the insight that through this hard-won self-awareness comes the awareness of the psychic reality, charged with an aura of the numinous, which Jung calls the self. Moreover, as I have suggested earlier, the self is a medium through which God makes his presence known to us and we become aware of him. The many today who are seeking a consciously realized union with God could find in some of the methods invented

5   *The Cloud of Unknowing*, ch. 14

for his psychotherapeutic work new and valuable tools to aid them.

One way in which an individual can use Jung's tools to awaken or deepen his awareness of God is by recalling and perhaps writing down and reflecting upon his dreams. Some forty years ago I had a dream which made a great impression upon me and which I have never forgotten. It was quite simple.

> I was standing on the edge of a large green field. In the centre of the field there was a tiny child crying his eyes out. I walked to the child, picked him up and did my best to comfort him without much success. He looked at me and said in a tearful voice, 'You can't do much good'.

At first I could make nothing of the dream. Then I supposed that the child represented a tendency to self-pity in myself which I was aware of. Further reflection made me think that he represented repressed sexuality as Freud would have said with much truth. Not till years later did it occur to me that the field with the child in the centre was a mandala symbol and was telling me of the great self of which my little ego was a part. Today the mental picture of the field with the child in the centre, not now weeping but happy, communicates a sense of inner security and strength. It speaks to me of a presence, not far away but within me.

It is necessary to mention one marked difference between Jung's language and that of the old spiritual guides. They understood self-awareness largely as becoming aware of sinful tendencies, whereas sin hardly has a place in the modern psychologist's vocabulary. The difference however is less than appears at first sight. For it is not so much sins whether of commission or omission, of wrong actions done or right actions left undone, with which *The Cloud* is concerned, but with the state or attitude of sinfulness. It bids us make ourselves aware of the deep-seated emotional disorder of our nature which is the seed-bed of our actual sins. Sin is a theological word which has to do with a breach in our relationship with God, and it cannot be rightly understood if taken out of that context. Jung is very well aware of the reality which the old spiritual guides call sin. The individuation process which requires a person to change his ways, to accept and give expression to elements in himself which he has been rejecting, encounters strong resistance. We are reluctant to give up the old habits and attitudes of mind which are familiar and give us a sense of security; and these reluctances block the change which is needed if our whole being is to find fulfilment. The resistances to change, the clinging desperately to the old and familiar, are just a secular way of describing what the old spiritual guides call sin.

The salvation which the Christian seeks differs from the individuation which Jung sees as the goal of human life but there is an overlap of meaning. For salvation, which must be understood in terms of oneness with God and his will, includes the individual's personal fulfilment in the life to come and some real anticipation of it in this life. Further Jung acknowledges individuation to be a rare achievement and beyond the reach of most people.

Another parallel between the process of individuation and the spiritual search for oneness with God can be seen at the very outset of both these adventures of the soul. At the beginning of the deliberate search for self-realization Jung places the confrontation with the shadow, the elements in an individual which he feels to be bad and to be rejected. This teaching resembles that of the old guides who insist that the spiritual novice must face and battle manfully with the image of sin within him, for this conflict is an essential part of the road to the knowledge of God. To become aware of God the individual must enter into the darkness within him, the unexplored hinterland of the personality, where dwell the unacceptable remains of childish narcissism and the repressed energies of aggression and the sex drive. The old masters insist that the experience of God is no mere intellectal knowledge. It is a heart-knowledge, in which emotion and instinct, intuition and the irrational, body as well as soul must participate. It is in line with this ancient wisdom that the spiritual guides of the Eastern Orthodox Churches describe true prayer as holding the mind in the heart.

Many people have recognized God's providence in their lives retrospectively, as they looked back into the past and traced the manner in which people and events had influenced them and directed their steps towards personal fulfilment, in ways unperceived at the time. Jung's teaching about the self and individuation can help the individual to perceive God's guiding action as a reality in the present. For the natural process of individuation which operates regardless of our own will, a process which we can try either to work with or to disregard, is an eloquent sign pointing to God's rule within our lives. Further this rule of God, which has often been felt to be restrictive and a hindrance to spontaneity, can be understood as directing us by inspiration from within and as opening up new and expanding possibilities. Jung's ideas can help to put a new complexion on obedience to God's will, which can be seen as an adventure in discovering and acting upon promptings which spring out of our deepest nature. The risks of the spiritual journey are largely just the hazards of daring to be oneself, of daring to follow the dictates of one's own individual truth. One of the rewards of the journey will be that of becoming more and more completely what one essentially is.

God guides the individual not only through the influence of the self, the total personality, upon his conscious thinking and planning but also through the world outside him. He guides him through other people, their friendship, their advice, their criticism, even their antagonism. He guides him not only through his contemporaries but also through a vast number of men and women now dead whose influence reaches him through their writings, their art and the institutions which they built. He guides the Christian through the Church, its scriptures and tradition, its worship, fellowship and sacraments. But this guidance from outside only becomes fully real and operative when it is checked and authenticated within our own being and in our actual experience.

The individuation process begins in the cradle and continues right up to the grave, to be completed, so the believer holds, in a life beyond death's river. Jung has much to say about the stages of life, each with its own landmarks, opportunities and dangers. The inborn urge of the individual to realize himself as much as possible carries him on a winding course. To explore the successive stages of life under the guidance of Jung will shed further light on the manner in which men and women experience God's guiding hand and face his summons to life.

4

GOD'S PROVIDENCE AND THE STAGES OF LIFE

The individuation process is the name given by Jung to a movement of maturing, which begins at birth or perhaps even earlier in the pre-natal life of the infant. In other words it is an element in human growth and development. It proceeds side by side with biological growth and becomes discernible when the individual has become mature enough to participate decisively in the process, as he must if individuation is to be achieved. The believer will see the movement towards individuation as one of the ways by which the Creator guides men and women towards their fulfilment. Jung has many illuminating observations about the stages which we pass through in the journey from the cradle to the grave. Reflection on these stages can help to make real the presence of God throughout the whole of life.

(i)

Jung compares human life with the course of the sun from its rising in the east to its setting in the west. Certain needs have to be met, certain tasks to be fulfilled in the morning of life, others in life's afternoon and evening. In the earliest phase of his life a child is wholly dependent on his parents. He is hardly conscious of himself as an independent individual; it is as though he were not completely born and were living in the psychic atmosphere of his parents. Self-consciousness becomes marked in adolescence when the uprush of sexual feeling and impulse disturbs the equilibrium of the growing boy and girl. Until this stage is reached the psychic life of the individual is largely governed by impulse and the social constraints of the family. He may be a problem to his parents but is not as a rule a problem to himself. His problems multiply as he grows from childhood into adolescence.

Jung sees the individual's life as divided into four main stages which might be termed childhood, youth, maturity and old age. The first two stages belong to life's dawn and morning, the last two to its afternoon and evening. It is the two long middle periods which particularly interest Jung, for life is then full of problems which as a doctor he wants to help people to solve.

On the subject of youth's problems Jung writes:

> If we try to extract the common and essential factors from the almost inexhaustible variety of individual problems found in the period of youth, we meet in nearly all cases with a particular feature: a more or less patent clinging to the childhood level of consciousness – a rebellion against the fateful forces in and around us which tend to involve us in the world. Something in us wishes to remain a child; to be unconscious, or, at most, only conscious of the ego; to reject everything foreign, or at least subject it to our will; to do nothing, or else indulge our own craving for pleasure or power.[1]

The forces of growth summon us to extend the horizon of life beyond the familiar world of home and school into the adult world of working for a living and of taking up responsibility for others as well as for ourselves and we resist this extension of consciousness. The enlargement of awareness begins long before adolescence. When at birth the child finds himself plunged into the strange and exciting world around him, a multitude of sense impressions stimulate him and cause his consciousness to expand. As he gradually acquires the power

1   *C.W.*, vol. viii, para. 764

of speech his curiosity lets loose a barrage of questions on parents and others. The enlargement of consciousness is further stimulated by school until it reaches a critical point at which problems have become so great that the individual begins to struggle against it:

> Achievement, usefulness and so forth are the ideals which seem to point the way out of the problematical state. They are the lodestars that guide us in the adventure of broadening and consolidating our physical existence; they help us to strike our roots in the world, but they cannot guide us in the development of that wider consciousness to which we give the name of culture. In the period of youth however this course is the normal one and in all circumstances preferable to tossing about in a welter of problems.[2]

At this stage the individual's progress is best made by concentrating on one of the possibilities which invite him and developing that successfully. This will mean neglecting other possibilities at least for a time. A person with some artistic ability may have to give up painting in order to earn his living in a bank or in accountancy. Sometimes an individual must 'scorn delights and live laborious days' if he is to gain a footing in the world of adult achievement. To restrict ourselves to the attainable and to neglect the ideal, however valid as a temporary measure, is never a lasting solution to our problems. Much of Jung's work as a doctor and psychotherapist consisted in helping people who had sacrificed too much of themselves in the struggle for success at this stage of early adulthood. All the same Jung insists on the necessity for this struggle and its importance for the individual:

> Of course to win for oneself a place in society and so to transform one's nature that it is more or less fitted to this existence, is in every instance an important achievement. It is a fight waged within oneself and outside comparable with the struggle of the child to defend his ego. The struggle is largely unobserved because it happens in the dark; but when we see how stubbornly childish illusions, presuppositions and egoistic habits are clung to in later years we are

2 Ibid., para. 769

able to realize the energy it took to form them. And so it is with the ideals, convictions, guiding ideas and attitudes which in the period of youth lead us into life – for which we struggle, suffer and win victories, they grow together with our own being, we apparently change into them, we seek to perpetuate them indefinitely and as a matter of course, just as the young person asserts his ego in spite of the world and often in spite of himself.[3]

As with the passage of years the individual advances from the morning of life to its afternoon a change of attitude becomes desirable and disturbing symptoms are likely to appear if he is unprepared for it. This mid-life situation is best described in Jung's own words:

> The nearer we approach to the middle of life and the better we have succeeded in entrenching ourselves in our personal attitudes and social positions, the more it appears as if we had discovered the right course and the right ideals and principles of behaviour. For this reason we suppose them to be eternally valid, and make a virtue of unchangeably clinging to them. We overlook the essential fact that the social goal is attained only at the cost of a diminution of personality. Many – far too many – aspects of life which should also have been experienced lie in the lumber room among dusty memories; but sometimes too they are glowing coals under grey ashes.[4]

> The very frequent neurotic disturbances of adult years all have one thing in common; they want to carry the psychology of the youthful phase over the threshold of the so-called years of discretion. Who does not know those touching old gentlemen who must always warm up the dish of their student days, who can fan the flame of life only by reminiscences of their heroic youth, but who for the rest are stuck in a hopelessly wooden Philistinism? As a rule, to be sure, they have this one merit which it would be wrong to undervalue: they are not neurotic but only boring and stereotyped. The neurotic is rather a person who can never

3   Ibid., para. 771
4   Ibid., para. 772

have things as he would like them in the present, and who can therefore never enjoy the past either.[5]

As formerly the neurotic could not part with his childhood so now he cannot part with his youth. He shrinks from the grey thoughts of approaching age, and, feeling the prospect before him unbearable, is always straining to look behind him. Just as the childish person shrinks back from the unknown in the world and in human existence, so the grown man shrinks back from the second half of life. It is as if unknown and dangerous tasks awaited him, or as if he were threatened with sacrifices and losses he does not wish to accept, or as if his life up to now seemed to him so fair and precious that he cannot relinquish it.[6]

Jung rejects as improbable the idea that this mid-life anxiety is at bottom the fear of death, for at that time death is seen as a distant and abstract-seeming event in the future. He likens human growth as we have seen to the course of a sun endowed with human feelings and man's limited consciousness. In the morning the sun rises from the night of unconsciousness and spreads its light and warmth over more and more of the world as it rises higher and higher in the sky. Then, at the stroke of noon the sun begins to descend. This descent means the reversal of the aims, values and ideals of the morning. Jung insists that the image of the rising and setting sun is not mere sentimental fairy-story. There is something sun-like within us, and to speak of the morning and evening, of the spring and autumn of life gives expression to psychological truths and even physiological facts:

Especially among southern races one can observe that older women develop deep rough voices, incipient moustaches, rather hard features and other masculine traits. On the other hand the masculine physique is toned down by feminine features, such as adiposity and softer facial expressions.[7]

5   Ibid., para. 776
6   Ibid., para. 777
7   Ibid., para. 780

Jung adds that the change is even more noticeable in the psychic sphere than in the physical. It often happens that a man in his late forties or early fifties winds up his business and busies himself with domestic chores or with the garden while his wife dons the trousers and opens up a little shop in which her husband can do odd jobs. Many women only wake up to their social responsibilities after they have passed their fortieth milestone. It is as though a man exhausts his masculine capacities in the first part of his life and allows his softer, more feminine feelings, which he had kept under before, to rule him. At the same time the more aggressive, masculine traits which a woman usually suppresses in her earlier years come to the fore as she grows older.

> The worst of it all is that intelligent and cultivated people live their lives without even knowing of the possibility of such transformations. Wholly unprepared, they embark upon the second half of life . . . Worse still we take this step with the false assumption that our truths and ideals will serve us as hitherto. But we cannot live the afternoon of life according to the programme of life's morning; for what was great in the morning will be little in the evening, and what in the morning was true will at evening have become a lie. I have given psychological treatment to too many people of advancing years, and have looked too often into the secret chambers of their souls, not to be moved by this fundamental truth.[8]

> Ageing people should know that their lives are not mounting and expanding, but that an inexorable inner process enforces the contraction of life. For a young person it is almost a sin, or at least a danger, to be too preoccupied with himself. After having lavished its light upon the world, the sun withdraws its rays in order to illuminate itself. Instead of doing likewise, many old people prefer to be hypochondriacs, niggards, pedants, applauders of the past or else eternal adolescents – all lamentable substitutes for the illumination of the self, but inevitable consequences of

8   Ibid., para. 784

the delusion that the second half of life must be governed by the principles of the first.[9]

Jung was convinced that the second half of life must have its own significance for the human species and should not be seen as a mere appendix to the pursuits and interests of the first half. Otherwise men and women would not go on living to seventy or eighty:

> The significance of the morning undoubtedly lies in the development of the individual, our entrenchment in the outer world, the propagation of our kind, and the care of our children. This is the obvious purpose of nature. But when this purpose has been attained – and more than attained – shall the earning of money, the extension of conquests and the expansion of life go steadily on beyond the bounds of all reason and sense? Whoever carries over into the afternoon the law of the morning, or the natural aim, must pay for it with damage to his soul, just as surely as a growing youth who tries to carry over his childish egoism into adult life must pay for this mistake with social failure. Money-making, social achievement, family and posterity are nothing but plain nature, not culture. Culture lies outside the purpose of nature. Could by any chance culture be the meaning and purpose of the second half of life?[10]

(ii)

Jung is convinced that the meaning of the second half of life is to be found in the service of culture in the broadest sense of the word. Culture then would include not only the arts – painting, sculpture, architecture, music and literature – but everything that broadens the mind and uplifts the spirit, everything that gives a transcendent meaning to life and especially religion. He remarks that: 'In primitive tribes we observe that the old people are almost always the guardians

9 Ibid., para. 785
10 Ibid., para. 787

of the mysteries and the laws, and it is in these that the cultural heritage of the tribe is expressed.'[11] Jung writes as a psychologist and doctor concerned with the psychic health of men and women. From this standpoint it is fatal for old people to look back in nostalgia to the past. To be healthy they must let go of the past and look forward to a goal in the future. He points out that all the great religions promise a life beyond this life, and that this hope enables people to live in the second half of life with as much purpose and perseverance as in the first. He does not try to prove that there is a life to come. He believes that there can be no scientific proof of this, nor indeed disproof. He writes:

> I have observed that a life directed to an aim is in general better, richer and healthier than an aimless one, and that it is better to go forwards with the stream of time than backwards against it. To a psychotherapist an old man who cannot bid farewell to life appears as feeble and as sickly as a young man who is unable to embrace it. And as a matter of fact, it is in many cases a question of the self-same childish greediness, the same fear, the same defiance and wilfulness, in the one as in the other. As a doctor I am convinced that it is hygienic – if I may use the word – to discover in death a goal towards which one can strive, that shrinking away from it is something unhealthy and abnormal, which robs the second half of life of its purpose. I therefore consider that all religions with a supramundane goal are eminently reasonable from the point of view of psychic hygiene. When I live in a house which I know will fall about my head within the next two weeks all my vital functions will be impaired by this thought; but if on the contrary I feel myself to be safe, I can dwell there in a normal and comfortable way. From the standpoint of psychotherapy it would therefore be desirable to think of death as only a transition, as a part of a life process whose extent and duration are beyond our knowledge.[12]

It is sometimes asserted that people cling to a belief in a life

11 Ibid., para. 788
12 Ibid., para. 792

to come because they are unwilling to face the harsh reality
of personal extinction. Jung suggests that the belief has much
more to do with the desire to live right up to the end with the
courage and serenity proper to man. He writes:

> In spite of the fact that the majority of people do not know
> why the body needs salt everyone demands it nonetheless
> because of an instinctive need. It is the same with the
> things of the psyche. By far the greater portion of mankind
> have from time immemorial felt the need of believing in a
> continuance of life. The demands of therapy, therefore, do
> not lead us into any by-paths but down the middle of the
> highway trodden by humanity. For this reason we are
> thinking correctly, and in harmony with life, even though
> we do not know what we think.[13]

Jung takes the view that the reality of the life to come, like
that of the existence of God, can neither be proved nor dis-
proved scientifically. His observations on the psychological
effect of belief in a future life indicate its relevance and importance. The Christian's faith in the life to come rests pri-
marily on his faith in God and in God's self-disclosure in
Christ. But the believer, though he relies on what he cannot
rationally prove, insists that his faith in no way contradicts
reason and is congruous with what can be known through
observation and rational reflection. And so he can be glad of
the reassurance that Jung brings that his faith is in agreement
with the needs of the psyche and is in no way alien to them.

Jung's teaching about the stages of life, taken as a broad
and general outline of the way things happen in life's journey,
I find convincing. Further, the inevitabilities that hedge the
individual in as he passes from life's morning to its afternoon
can bring home to the believer the inescapable reality of
God's guiding presence in his life. It can also better enable
him to co-operate with God's leading. The kind of religious
discipline valuable in the first half of life may need to be
modified if not totally changed in the second half. The methods of prayer which served us well in the early stages may be
quite unsuitable later on. Forewarned is forearmed, and the

13 Ibid., para. 793

awareness of what is bound to take place will leave us less disconcerted when we find that old ideals have faded and old ways of prayer have lost their sense of meaning.

Jung was well aware that life is not so tidy as his scheme seems to suggest. There are many complicating factors. Sometimes an individual for a variety of reasons may fail to fulfil the tasks of the morning and so perforce, if his life is not to be wholly stultified, must learn to fulfil them in the afternoon when the time is less favourable. Sometimes when an individual is well advanced in years there comes a late flowering of unsuspected talents which for one reason or another had lain dormant. Often the demands of society which in favourable circumstances should encourage an individual's growth to maturity hamper and even cripple it.

(iii)

People differ widely and an individual's course through life will be affected by his temperamental make-up. Jung's analysis of differing types of individual sheds light on the varying fortunes of people whose home background and upbringing is similar. A brief look at the way in which Jung understands these differences will shed further light on the complexities of human nature and the divine ordering of our lives.

Jung's division of people into extraverts and introverts is widely known and accepted by many who differ from him in their psychological standpoint. Jung writes:

> There is a whole class of men who at the moment of reaction to a given situation at first draw back a little as if with an unvoiced 'no', and only after that are able to react; and there is another class who in the same situation come forward with an immediate reaction, apparently confident that their behaviour is obviously right . . . The former class corresponds to the introverted and the second to the extraverted attitude.[14]

Jung speaks of the introverted and extraverted attitudes.

14 *C.W.*, vol. vi, para. 937

Everyone can react in either of these ways and an individual is called an introvert or extravert when the one or the other attitude has become predominant or habitual. There appears to be a physiological basis for the two types though environmental influences no doubt play their part.

The introvert and the extravert are likely to follow different courses in their journey through life even when they have similar starting points. Jung writes:

> The earliest mark of extraversion in a child is his quick adaptation to the environment, and the extraordinary attention he gives to objects, especially to his effect upon them. Shyness in regard to objects is very slight; the child moves and lives among them with trust. He makes quick perceptions, but in a haphazard way. Apparently he develops more quickly than an introverted child, since he is less cautious and, as a rule, has no fear. Apparently too he feels no barrier between himself and objects, and hence he can play with them freely and learn through them. He gladly pushes his undertakings to an extreme and risks himself in the attempt. Everything unknown seems alluring.[15]

Parents and teachers like this sort of child who tends to be open, responsive and teachable. The introvert child tends to be shy and cautious in his attitude both to objects and to people. Introvert children are happy to play by themselves and prefer to have one or two friends rather than the many friends which the extravert tends to acquire. The introvert may be just as gifted intellectually or artistically as the extravert, but is likely to develop more slowly and to find it harder to gain recognition. This latter is partly due to the fact that the modern world tends to value the extravert type more than the introvert. Extraverts are better adjusted to the external world and to society than introverts; but in responding to the expectations of others they may easily do violence to the deeper needs of their own nature. On the other hand the introvert who has much greater difficulty in forming relations with others is much more in touch with his own inner feelings

15 Ibid., para. 896

and intuitions and will avoid if at all possible doing violence to them. The great disaster for the extravert would be to be excluded from the society of his fellows, that for the introvert would be to be so dominated by society that he was unable to call his soul his own. In the morning of life extraverts usually have a big advantage over introverts; for this is the time when it is of the utmost importance to break free from the parent-dominated world of childhood and establish themselves in the adult world of work and social responsibility. Their outgoing nature will lead them to welcome the stimulus of an expanding world and adjust themselves to it without difficulty. This is likely to be much more difficult for the introvert whose tendency is to be reserved and shy and afraid to commit himself. In the morning of life the introvert will probably need much encouragement if he is to carry out successfully the tasks which belong to that period. In life's afternoon the situation is likely to be reversed. The extravert has probably adjusted himself to the world all too well, and is likely to find impossibly difficult the afternoon's task of loosening his hold on his external life and interests in order to attend to the needs of his neglected inner life. At this later stage the extravert will tend to be more in need of help than his introvert brother or sister.

It is self-evident that people vary not only in their tendency to adopt an introvert or extravert attitude to life but in a host of other ways. Jung lists four functions or modes by which we can handle the people and problems that meet us – sensation, thinking, feeling and intuition. He divides people according to which of these functions they tend to rely on most, the function which for that reason tends to be most fully developed. Jung writes:

> Just as the lion strikes down his enemy or his prey with his fore-paw in which his strength resides, and not with his tail like the crocodile, so our habitual reactions are normally characterized by the application of our most trustworthy and efficient function; it is an expression of our strength. However this does not prevent us from reacting occasionally in a way that reveals our specific weakness. The predominance of a function leads us to construct or seek out

certain situations while we avoid others, and therefore to have experiences which are peculiar to ourselves and different from those of other people. An intelligent man will make his adaptation to the world through his intelligence, and not in the manner of a sixth-rate pugilist, even though now and then in a fit of anger he may make use of his fists. In the struggle for existence and adaptation everyone instinctively uses his most developed function.[16]

Jung calls two of the four functions, sensation and intuition, perceptive functions, because they are concerned with facts. Sensation – seeing, hearing, touching, tasting – fastens on to the immediate physical facts around us. Frieda Fordham writes:

> The sensation type takes everything as it comes, experiences things as they are, no more and no less; no imagination plays around his experiences, no thought attempts to look deeper into them or explore their mysteries – a spade is a spade; neither is any real valuation made; what counts is the strength and pleasure of the sensation.[17]

Intuition like sensation is a perceptive function, but it is concerned not so much with the facts themselves, which it finds too obvious to be interesting, but the facts behind the facts, the possibilities hidden in them. Jung defines intuition as perception through the unconscious. The individual exercising intuition is like someone standing on the shore of the unconscious and unknown waiting to see what its waves and tides will throw up on to the beach of consciousness. In situations of darkness and perplexity intuition by a kind of inspired guessing often perceives the way forward when no amount of reasoning could have discovered it. Sensation and intuition are opposites and tend to exclude each other. The person who relies on sensation concentrates on the facts under his nose and dismisses the possibilities the other side of the hill as just idle speculation. The intuitive on the other hand is inclined to overlook the obvious facts and is concerned to

16 Ibid., para. 947
17 *An Introduction to Jung's Psychology* (Penguin Books 1953), p. 42

perceive what they are pointing to; he looks not at the surface of a statement but what may lie behind it.

The other two functions, thinking and feeling, are termed by Jung rational or judging functions. Thinking judges opinions or statements as true or false, feeling judges people, things and ideas as good or bad, attractive or unattractive. Jung's idea of feeling is difficult to grasp because in ordinary English usage the word denotes not only feeling in Jung's sense but also both sensation and intuition. For example to say 'This water feels hot' is to use feeling to refer to sensation, or to say 'I feel there is more in this than meets the eye' is to use feeling to refer to intuition. Jung limits feeling to the acknowledgement of value as in the sentence 'I feel this is right'. It is especially in the field of personal relationships that feeling is important. Our feelings lead us to approve some people and disapprove of others, to incline to certain actions as right and away from others as wrong. The warm and sympathetic individual is usually one who relies greatly on feeling. Like sensation and intuition thinking and feeling are opposites. The intellectual or thinking type desires to reason things out clearly and tends to regard the intrusion of feelings of pleasure or dislike as a distracting interference with his effort to form a reasonable judgement. He often makes a point of setting out facts without making any value judgements upon them. The feeling type sees this attitude of cold judgement-free detachment, especially in regard to matters of great human concern, as a deplorable want of humanity.

The four functions in their different ways all help us to cope with our world. Through sensation we take careful note of facts, through thinking we try to understand the facts rationally; feeling judges the facts as good or bad, attractive or unattractive, and through intuition we look beyond the bare facts to what lies behind them and what they may lead to. Of course in practice we face and react to situations using instinctively whatever function seems appropriate without reflecting on what we are doing. But in actual fact, as has been pointed out, we tend to rely on one or two functions rather than all of them equally, with the result that the constantly used functions tend to be well developed and under control, while the underdeveloped functions tend to be used clumsily.

Jung's scheme greatly over-simplifies a complex, not to say highly mysterious matter, as he well understood. It disregards many important human variables, such as the enormous differences in intelligence, practical ability and drive between individuals, and, further, the effects of widely differing social background and upbringing. But if due allowance is made for these as well as for the essential uniqueness and mysteriousness of every human personality, the analysis can shed some light on life's tasks, difficulties and opportunities.

In the first half of life an individual, if he is reasonably fortunate, will most probably develop his strongest functions as he seeks to establish himself in a career or learn to master a job. But in the second half of life it will be important to let some of the talents or interests, perforce neglected in the morning, come into operation in the afternoon. Sometimes a hobby can provide a channel along which a hitherto unused stream of energy and initiative can flow, bringing to the individual a sense of freedom and deep satisfaction. We live in an age of specialization which though valuable to the community can be damaging to the individual. For this reason it is important to take steps to counteract the narrowing effect of work or of a manner of life which keeps too much of an individual's humanity suppressed. Belief that God is behind these natural processes of development can provide the individual with a strong incentive to break out of the rut into which society has forced him and to develop his unused gifts and talents to the best of his ability. He can see this as part of his commitment to his Creator.

(iv)

Another factor in the growth of personality needs to be looked at before this chapter ends. It springs out of the inevitable conflict between what an individual is or feels himself to be and what society expects him to be. This tension between the individual and society begins in infancy and continues through life. The child in order to meet his parents' wishes and conform to their rules has to give up many childish desires. It is part of the civilizing process that everyone has to go through. We all have to suppress something of ourselves in order to be acceptable to society. In practice the individual learns to adopt a manner, to wear a kind of psychological mask, which is a compromise between what we really are and want and what will make a favourable impression on others. Jung calls this mask the *persona*, a word taken from ancient Roman and Greek drama, referring to the mask an actor wore, to signify the character he was playing, in the large open air theatres of the ancient world where the actor's features could not easily be distinguished. We are all forced by society to play a role, to assume a persona which both expresses and conceals what we are. As Jung writes:

> Society expects and indeed must expect every individual to play the part assigned to him as perfectly as possible, so that a man who is a parson must not only carry out his official duties objectively, but must at all times and in all circumstances play the role of a parson in a flawless manner. Society demands this as a kind of surety; each must stand at his post, here a cobbler, there a poet. No man is expected to be both. Such a man would be 'different' from other people, not quite reliable. In the academic world he would be a dilettante, in politics an 'unpredictable' quantity, in religion a free-thinker – in short, he would always be suspected of unreliability and incompetence, because society is persuaded that only the cobbler who is not a poet can supply workmanlike shoes.[18]

The doctor, the lawyer, the priest, the shop assistant, the policeman, all play roles; society expects this of them. We should most of us be disturbed to see a group of policemen in uniform playing football in the street.

So far we have considered professional roles, but there are a great many semi-private roles which we adopt – that of the host or hostess, for example, or of the sympathetic acquaintance. The roles we play inevitably clash, sometimes severely, with our deepest feelings. This can be acutely painful when, for example, under the stress of bereavement we have to carry on with our ordinary work. Yet at the same time the role is

18 *C.W.*, vol. vii, para. 305

a protection, for it helps to conceal our secret anxiety or resentment from the casual eye of every Tom, Dick and Harry. It can enable us to fulfil our social obligations in spite of being weighed down by moods of anger or despair. A role or persona is useful to an individual if he is able to discard it whenever it is inappropriate. It can be a handicap to anyone who is so identified with his role that he cannot lay it aside when circumstances make it wholly unsuitable. The judge who on all occasions is issuing judgements, the schoolteacher who is always instructing others, the counsellor who must be always giving advice, are examples of over-identification with a role. The pompous person is one who on all occasions is trying to play a dignified role and so in fact frequently makes himself ridiculous. When a persona has become so fixed that the individual sees himself as wholly identified with it, then the real person must wither and diminish. The extravert finds it easier than the introvert to develop the kind of persona which will enable him to adapt himself to society and to succeed in a career. But just for that reason in the second half of life he is likely to find it more difficult than the introvert to lay aside the social attitude which has stood him in such good stead and so allow the suppressed or neglected side of his nature to expand and bring about a release of new life in him.

Jung's account of the stages of life, his analysis of human types and his description of the persona leave an immense amount unexplained. They should be seen as providing a set of mental tools for the better understanding of the multitudinous variety of human beings and the problems and difficulties they encounter as they pursue their course through life. Their greatest value will be found in the light they can shed on the road our own lives have taken. For it is only as I learn to recognize the real nature of my own problems and perceive more clearly the nature and cause of my own past blunders that I shall begin to understand the individuals, unique and mysterious, whom I meet. Further I find my own faith in God strengthened as I trace the way in which God steers men and women through life's morning and afternoon, in such a way as to enable them to grow wise in the realization of their own truth and so get ready for the voyage into endless life.

The stages of life which we pass through on the human journey are part of the individuation process. This ongoing development of the psyche is complicated by the presence of forces both within and outside the individual which hinder and block it, the presence in a word of evil. In trying to explain this troublesome reality Jung makes use of the concept, already referred to, of the shadow. We shall need to examine this concept further in order to see what light, if any, it can shed on the Christian belief about sin and redemption.

5

THE SHADOW AND THE REDEEMER

The individuation process as it advances through life's successive stages and leads the individual to fuller life and greater authenticity is no smooth and easy progress. It is punctuated by crises caused by obstacles and hindrances, arising either from outer circumstance or inner fears, which dam the psychic energy and impede the forward flow of the life-stream. In other words human life is under threat from destructive forces or evil. It was one of Jung's complaints against Christian theologians that they did not take evil seriously enough. In particular he took violent exception to the doctrine taught by the fifth-century St Augustine that evil is *privatio boni*, the absence of good, just as darkness is the absence of light. I think with Victor White, who had long arguments with him on the subject, that Jung, who was neither a theologian nor a philosopher, misunderstood the doctrine and that the very positive qualities of evil which Jung emphasized did not contradict it. However this may be, Jung saw evil as a powerful fact and it seemed to him that his Christian contemporaries failed to come to terms with its dangerous reality.

(i)

Jung uses the idea of the shadow to explain what he means by evil. The shadow is caused by light, for where there is no light there can be no shadow. As the individual grows up he faces the tasks which his own nature and society's expectations impose upon him with the help of aims and ideals, partly offered by society, partly chosen by himself. In pursuit of his personal aim the individual tries to ignore or reject impulses and emotions which conflict with it and in doing so builds up an attitude which represents partly what he aspires to become, partly what he sees himself to be and wishes others so to see him. For example, part of an individual's ideal might be to act courageously, to face up to difficulty and danger without evasion or running away. In pursuit of that ideal he says 'no' to the feeling of fear and the impulse to run away and forces himself to act firmly and with fortitude. In time it may become habitual to him to repress fear so that he may even become totally oblivious of the warning impulses signalling danger; they have become unconscious. For the fear that I refuse to acknowledge does not cease to exist, it lives on within me, buried out of sight. Sensitivity to danger is something deeply ingrained in us, inherited from a million ancestors human and pre-human, and cannot be banished by an effort of will.

Jung calls the rejected elements of the personality the shadow. The whole-hearted following of the ideal of fearlessness inevitably causes growth of its opposite in the unconscious, as a bright light must cause a shadow when it falls upon an opaque object. This shadow element is by no means wholly passive. It makes its influence felt in disconcerting ways, like a child who ignored by grown-ups makes a nuisance of himself in order to attract attention. One of the ways in which the shadow forces itself upon the attention of the conscious personality is dreams in which it may appear as a beggar difficult to shake off or some disreputable relative who tags on to you or perhaps a thug who is out for your life. The more determined a person is in pursuit of his ideal the darker will its opposite be, just as the brighter the light the darker the shadow it will cast. Most people are not so whole-hearted in the following of an ideal as to be able to repress all the feelings and impulses that conflict with it. Usually we are at least intermittently aware of them. But if I do manage to repress the shadow side of my personality completely a curious thing happens. I project my shadow on to someone else, probably of my own sex. I shall see another person as the embodiment of all that I dislike and despise in myself. So the shadow succeeds in calling attention to itself in this disguised form. I shall see the other person as the personification of what is shifty, cowardly and evasive. He will arouse in me dislike and animosity, perhaps fear. I shall find it impossible to be fair to him, for without knowing it I am using him as a peg on which to hang and objectify just those qualities that I am unable to accept in myself. There must be something about him that makes him a suitable peg, but I shall be blind to all his other qualities and he is likely to become my *bête noire*. He is unbearable to me because he stands for something in myself which I do not wish to own. He also enables me to maintain a good opinion of myself because he carries my rejected bad qualities which otherwise I might have to acknowledge as my own. I have described an extreme case. Our aims and ideals are mixed and we are seldom able to dismiss from our consciousness all our undesirable qualities; and these nag us with a feeling of guilt. But no one is without a shadow, and something like what I have described occurs to some degree in all people.

A dream I had some thirty-five years ago gives a striking illustration of the shadow. I had been under a great deal of pressure from work and had just conducted two retreats one after the other. This had involved my giving a number of addresses which, through no real fault of mine, had been inadequately prepared. My dream was as follows:

> An unpleasant looking man was driving a cart in which were a lot of small children. The man stopped the cart and then proceeded to seize each child by the legs and bash his head on the ground. There were ten of them, all dead. I was horrified and woke up.

At first I could make nothing of the dream, but the number ten held my attention. What could it refer to? It then slowly dawned on me that I had given precisely ten addresses in the two retreats. The dream was telling me that I had murdered ten potentially good addresses. It was also calling my attention to a disagreeable and ruthless element in myself which I had been blind to, my shadow.

There is not only the personal shadow, the elements in myself which I have rejected because they clash with my personal ideal. There is also the collective or archetypal shadow, the obverse of the collective ideal of mankind or, more specifically, of my nation, culture or class. Every nation has an idea of what a man or woman should be which differs slightly from that of other nations. The English ideal is not precisely the same as the Scottish, Irish, French or American ideal, to say nothing of that of the Arab or Hindu. As we grow up we automatically imbibe through our home and parents, through school, literature and the mass media the ideals of our nation and class and tend to despise and reject what conflicts with them. The heroes of boys' books of seventy years ago assumed the superiority of English men and women and the inferiority of other races. The heroes of those books might be displayed defending with the help of a few chosen companions a stockade against the attack of savage and cruel warriors who greatly outnumbered them, taking a deadly toll with their accurate shooting. Racial arrogance often blinded the white pioneer in his skirmishes with hostile native tribes to the fact that he himself was the aggressor and had no moral right to seize the land and disrupt the lives of native Africans for his own advantage. By repressing their greed and aggression and projecting it on to the natives they were able to see themselves as civilizing benefactors.

Perhaps the most striking illustration of the sinister power of the collective shadow in this century is the mass extermination of six million Jews at the orders of Adolf Hitler, already referred to. We cannot understand the rise of the Nazis to power in Germany if we do not see it as in part the effect of an ideal, the perverted ideal of a master race, a race of heroes. It was this ideal proclaimed by its prophet Hitler which swept Germany like wildfire. Not only were the imaginations of the young captivated by the vision of a greater Germany but most of the middle-aged and elderly too, including scholars, scientists and theologians. It seemed at first to many observers outside Germany that the nation was being regenerated. Not only was unemployment abolished but the young, boys and girls, men and women, were fired by the ambition to live heroically and, if need be, shed their blood for the fatherland. But we do not become heroic in a moment. Our meanness, evasiveness and cowardice are not spirited away when we embrace an heroic ideal. These qualities are repressed and, however unwilling we may be to admit it, live on in our unconscious and exercise a disturbing influence on our conduct. Unless this shadow side is acknowledged it will undermine and corrupt our ideal. All this Hitler understood instinctively. And so he encouraged the projection of all evil, of everything mean and unheroic, on to the Jews, whom he represented as the embodiment of everything shifty and un-German. He was able to do this partly because there was a long tradition of Jew hating and Jew baiting, and not only in Germany. But it is important to see the inhuman persecution of the Jews as the shadow cast by the uncritical, indeed the fanatical, following of an ideal. Perhaps we could sum up the danger of a collective ideal as that of falling into idolatry: that is the giving of supreme value to a good which is real but limited. Patriotism is not enough; it is good but it is not the supreme good.

If we look to Germany under Hitler for the most conspicuous recent example of the power for evil of the collective shadow we can see its presence at work everywhere. The intractable problems of Ulster and the Middle East can both be seen as due to the clash of ideals erected into absolutes, which makes reasonable concession and compromise impossible. An example of this in our own country is the National Front movement. The ideal behind the movement is patriotism, but there is an element of fanaticism which, though in a less virulent form, is reminiscent of the Nazi sickness. Not Jews but black people are made the scapegoat upon which are projected our national faults and weaknesses. When we project our own shadow side on to others we render ourselves incapable of seeing them as ordinary human beings with good points and bad, just like ourselves. Another possible example is the festival of light movement, whose goal is the raising of moral standards, an impeccable ideal it would seem. Unfortunately some of the adherents of the movement pursue their goal with a fanaticism which blinds them to what is good in the so-called permissive society, which they condemn. For, granted that the moral irresponsibility of many today is something to be deplored as bad, indeed anti-human, yet the non-judgemental character of contemporary ideals and the respect for human freedom are good. As we have seen, when I project my shadow or some aspect of it on to another individual or class of individuals, they become the stereotype of what I fear, despise or dislike in myself. I am able to maintain a good opinion of myself because what contradicts my self-image is projected on to others; the disapproval which I should otherwise have felt of myself is deflected on to them.

(ii)

Jung's teaching about the shadow sheds light on an important part of the gospel. In its original form the Christian message included a summons to repent and believe. The word 'repent' translates a Greek word, 'metanoeite', which means, literally, change your minds. Jung's teaching illuminates what this involves. Repentance has to do with change, change of direction, change of heart, change of attitude. But this change will not be brought about simply by embracing a new and better ideal, for a new ideal might simply help us to repress our shadow, the things we do not wish to acknowledge in ourselves. Repentance must indeed involve a conscious and deliberate choice, but it can only become effective as an inner change and renewal in our feelings and desires is brought about. Further, the choice involved in repentance cannot be a once-for-all decision but needs to be renewed daily by an effort to co-operate with God as he brings about a change in our emotions and desires. There is a long tradition which stresses the value of self-examination, in order to uncover the sins, failures and inconsistencies which contradict the following of Christ and the love of God and neighbour. Jung's teaching about the shadow can make possible a sharper and more searching self-examination.

The shadow as Jung understands it is never pure evil. It always contains much that is potentially good and indeed necessary for the individual's full development, his individuation. The threatening feelings which arise from our rejected shadow side, however opposed to our conscious aims, are not simply bad; rather they are the expression of elements of our personality which though undeveloped and distorted are, at least in principle, capable of being restored and put right. The natural sex drive if repressed from fear of its seductive strength may take on the character of lust, but if accepted it can become a source of vigour and delight in the marriage relationship and the building of a home. It can also infuse warmth into all human relationships. The natural instinct of self-preservation and self-affirmation, which if repressed through fear may express itself in impulses of ruthless ambition, could if accepted and owned for what it is supply the energy and drive for a life of responsible service in a career or in work for the common good. But how in practice do we learn to accept our shadow side without giving rein to its destructive potential?

An example will illustrate the problem. I want to take seriously my Christian obligation to live by the teaching of Christ and follow his example. I recall that Christ said that he came not to be served but to serve and that he urged his disciples to serve one another. Accordingly I embrace the ideal of service; I make up my mind to serve other people, to put their interests before my own, in conversation to listen to what others have to say and to be reticent in obtruding my own ideas. But directly I set out to act in this way I become aware of a violent rebellion within myself. I feel an immense desire to have my own way, I am filled with critical thoughts about others, I inwardly burn with anger at some imagined or unintended slight. I try to crush the self-assertive impulses in order to conform to my chosen ideal of service; I pray for the grace of humility. But what I may be really wanting in this prayer is either the power to keep under my self-assertive impulses or to have them magicked away. I examine my conscience and ask forgiveness for my pride and self-assertiveness. If I am very determined I may, so far as my words and actions are concerned, manage to appear humble and unobtrusive, but this is only an outward façade which the perceptive will easily see through. My inner feelings are far from humble; rather they are angry, resentful and sad. I am battling unsuccessfully with my shadow, the darkness caused by the light of my ideal.

Despite St Paul's very different terminology I believe that the experience of conflict with sin which he describes in his letter to the Romans can be understood and illuminated by Jung's idea of the shadow. 'I do not do the good I want, but the evil I do not want is what I do. Now if I do what I do not want, it is no longer I that do it but sin which dwells within me.'[1] The sin which dwells in a person is precisely what Jung personifies as the shadow. It acts like a sub-personality gathering to itself despised and rejected elements inconsistent with the individual's ideal, and is liable to push itself into the driving seat of the personality and take temporary control. But let us continue with St Paul's account and see how he comes to terms with the shadow, the indwelling sin. 'Wretched man that I am', he writes, 'Who shall deliver me from this body of death? Thanks be to God through Jesus Christ our Lord.'[2] The deliverance came, no doubt, through his vision on the road to Damascus and the voice which told him that Jesus, the despised and rejected Jew who had been put to death on a cross and whose disciples he had been persecuting, was the Lord.[3] Christ was able to heal the division within St Paul because he spoke with absolute authority to each of the opposed forces within, both the despised and rejected elements in his personality and the strong ethical ideals which had led to their rejection. Allegiance to Christ and trust in him brought unity in place of division and peace after conflict. He experienced a flooding in of love, joy and peace which he ascribes sometimes to the Holy Spirit, sometimes to Christ dwelling in him. St Paul understands the Christian life as a life closely identified with the crucified and rejected Christ. 'All of us who have been baptized into Christ Jesus were baptized into his death.'[4] 'I have been crucified with Christ; it is no longer I who live, but Christ who lives in me.'[5] Plainly St Paul is not thinking of a literal crucifixion;

1   Rom. 7:19–20
2   Rom. 7:24
3   Acts 9:1–9
4   Rom. 6:3
5   Rom. 7:24–25

he is using a powerful metaphor to describe the close identi-
fication of the believer with Christ's weakness and vulnerability. St Paul sees his old ego-directed life as ended and a
new life directed by a power within him begun. The faith or
trust which St Paul insists on as the way to salvation includes
the acceptance of weakness, of vulnerability, which is the
mark of the genuine disciple. It is not to be supposed that the
change brought about by trusting in Christ is instantaneous.
A decision to trust may be made in a split second, but the
implementation of the decision must take time. Old habits
and mental attitudes live on long after the reasons and the
circumstances which led to their formation have disappeared.
A new vision and purpose is liable to fail until it has led to
the building of new attitudes and habits which embody and
support it. As an individual learns step by step to trust more
and more of the outcast elements of his personality to the
power of Christ, once despised and rejected but now endowed
with absolute authority, these elements tend to change their
character until eventually, not without alarms and apparent
relapses, they become his allies rather than his enemies; they
play a necessary part in his progress on the road to self-
fulfilment.

Before leaving the subject of the shadow let us consider
what light Jung's teaching can shed on the traditional Christian practice of self-examination. It will emphasize the importance of bringing to light so far as possible not only our
conscious lapses and failures, but the unacceptable things in
ourselves of which we are unconscious and know only through
their effects. This will mean a kind of questioning designed
to probe the underground movements of subversion at work
in our thoughts, feelings and actions, a questioning designed
to enlarge self-awareness. Why did I forget that appointment?
Perhaps because I was afraid of the demands it might make
on my time and patience. Why did that piece of news cast
me into such a mood of depression? Perhaps because it seemed
to threaten some secret and unadmitted ambition. Why did
I feel so angry at the remark my boss made? Perhaps because
I am more dependent on his approval than I like to admit.
Why did I feel so hurt when my friend cried off from the

meeting we had arranged? Perhaps because I am much more jealous than I had thought.

The effect of this kind of self-examination is to modify our too flattering self-image by bringing home to us our frailty and weakness. If we believe in God as our strength in weakness and our wisdom in perplexity self-examination will drive us to turn to him. The fact of our vulnerability will be driven home and we shall realize that our one hope is in God. This paradoxically will bring a sense of peace. 'He that is low need fear no fall.' One of the fruits of self-awareness is humility.

Another effective means of coming 'to know and feel ourselves as we are' is to learn from our projections. I referred earlier to the psychological fact of projection, the tendency to read into others much that is in actual fact in ourselves. By learning to recognize when I am doing this I can make valuable discoveries about my own personality. Of course the dislike or irritation that another arouses in me does not necessarily imply that I am projecting on to him things that I dislike in myself. What convinces me of my projection is the irrational strength of my feelings and my inability to get rid of them. Directly I realize that I am projecting my own anger or fear on to another I am able to withdraw my projection and my dislike or resentment begins to fade. I read once of a woman who was very angry with her sister-in-law at some action of hers. As she lay in bed at night she could not sleep for dwelling on the incident that rankled. She argued the case in her mind and proved to herself that her sister-in-law had behaved abominably. Round and round in her head the argument ran making sleep impossible. Suddenly, during a pause in the inner dialogue, she heard a still small voice saying: 'The defendant has admirably stated the case for her own prosecution.' She sat up startled, she reflected and then it slowly dawned upon her that she had herself behaved in exactly the way she was blaming in her sister-in-law. With this access of self-knowledge her projection was withdrawn, her resentment evaporated and she fell asleep at peace. It must be added that to withdraw a projection is often a slow and arduous task. But to face and own our own shadow is the road to self-realization. The cell of self-knowledge is the place where alone, despite the discomfort to our self-esteem, we shall find lasting security.

Jung regards the facing and coming to terms with the personal shadow as the first step to be taken by anyone who wishes to co-operate with the individuation process. It resembles the *metanoia*, the change of heart, with which the believer responds to the gospel. But self-knowledge alone is not enough. Indeed the awareness of my selfish and possibly criminal tendencies might drive me to despair, if I had not grounds, like St Paul, for trusting a power greater than my own will to bring order out of my inner chaos. The power, according to Jung, which can bring order out of the conflict and confusion within is the living symbol. The reason for the ineffectiveness of my good intentions and deliberate efforts is the rebellion of my largely unknown and unacknowledged hopes and fears, ambitions and lusts. There is a gulf between my rational will and my archetypal instincts, between my head and my heart. This gulf is bridged by the living symbol. Let us look at what Jung means by symbol.

Jung has said of the symbol:

> By a symbol I do not mean an allegory or a sign, but an image which describes in the best possible way the dimly discerned nature of the spirit. A symbol does not define or explain; it points beyond itself to a meaning that is darkly divined but is still beyond our grasp, and cannot be adequately expressed in the familiar words of our language.[6]

The symbol belongs to two worlds, the world of every day and the inner world of the unconscious. We can reflect upon a symbol, we can amplify its meaning by recalling ideas associated with it, we can try to analyse it, or we can just contemplate it and try to open ourselves to the impact it makes upon us; but we can never grasp it fully, for it is rooted in the unconscious and draws its power from the archetypal energies that it activates within us. Writing of the power of symbols Jung states:

6 *C.W.*, vol. viii, para. 644

The most obvious and best example of this is the effectiveness of the Christian symbols, whose power changed the face of history. If one looks without prejudice at the way the spirit of early Christianity worked on the mind of the average man of the second century, one can only be amazed.[7]

There is a reservoir of psychic energy within men and women which cannot be tapped by will-power alone. Only the living symbol can lead it out and make it available to the conscious personality. Jung compares the symbol to the giant turbines which transform the weight of water that flows over the Niagara Falls into power, light and heat. Just so the living symbol by focusing the imagination releases the instinctive archetypal energy and emotion and so empowers action. Religion is powerful through its symbols, through images and figures, personal and impersonal, that stir men and women to their depths. For the living symbol liberates the spiritual energy latent within and guides it into the service of the values which religion upholds.

The central Christian symbol is, of course, Jesus Christ. The Christian believes him to be much more than a symbol, to be an actual person who lived and died and is alive still. But it is because he is able to be for men and women a living symbol that he is able to change their lives. In the case of St Paul, referred to earlier, the image of Jesus Christ, crucified but alive, released in him a spiritual energy that made him the foremost missionary of his time and perhaps of any time. The Christian sees in Christ the embodied symbol of the Creator, of the mystery behind and above and within all that exists. It is because the divine mystery has been brought near to mankind in the flesh and blood of a human life which culminated in the flesh and blood of a human death, that Christ is able to liberate his fellow humans for their true fulfilment.

It would be truer to say not that Christ is a symbol but that in him many archetypal symbols meet and merge. We can see this taking place in the New Testament. The actual

7   Ibid., loc. cit.

form that the archetypal images take is determined in any particular culture in part by its historical antecedents. We can see in the New Testament how the images that gripped the minds of the prophets and writers of the Old Testament are fused and focused in the person of Christ and in the minds of the New Testament writers. To quote again the theologian and biblical scholar, Austin Farrer:

> There had arisen in Judaism the image of heroic and un-merited suffering for God's glory and the good of the breth-ren, especially in the figure of Joseph: and this image was tending to fuse with that of the blood-offering in atonement for sin. There was also the image of the Messiah, in whose enthronement the Kingdom of God would be manifested on earth. There were also the images of the divine power and presence – God is in heaven, but his 'Name' is in the temple, his Wisdom or Word or Spirit is in the mind of the prophet or, in some degree, wherever there is a mind alive with the divine law. There was an image of divine sonship, belonging primarily to the chosen people. In Christ's very existence all these images fused. Joseph the saint of sacri-ficial loving-kindness, the ritual Lamb of the atonement, David the Viceroy of God, the Word of God's presence and power, Israel the Son of God, Adam the new created Image of God; all these were reborn in one divine Saviour out of the sepulchre of Christ.[8]

We see further the power of the figure of Christ to fulfil many archetypal themes if we reflect on a symbol not found in the Bible though dear to countless numbers of Christians, the crucifix. A number of ancient symbols meet and mingle in that thorn-crowned figure. The crucified Christ fulfils the age-old dream of the ideal king, the king who is the protector and guardian of his people, who leads his armies in battle and falls fighting for them, the martyr king. He is also the *Christus Victor*, the victorious Leader who by dying overcomes his people's enemies and by his resurrection turns a sign of ignominy into a symbol of glory. In the crucified we see also the innocent victim, the scapegoat that bears his people's sins,

8   Farrer, *Rebirth of Images*, p. 15

the Lamb of God through whose sacrifice sinful men and women are forgiven and reconciled to God. He is also the *Christus humilis*, the meek and lowly Christ, with arms stretched wide and head bowed, the Christ who summons the weary and heavy laden to come to him and find rest; the Christ whose weakness and vulnerability heals the wounds of pride and self-assertiveness and the insecurity which is the soil in which pride and self-assertiveness grow. Perhaps the most universal way of understanding the crucifix is as a window through which we can look into the mind and heart of God.

It would be possible to list many more images by means of which the unseen reality of Christ has been grasped and allowed to reverberate deep within the souls of those who believe in him. To take one pregnant sentence from St John's Gospel.[9] Christ is the Way, the road stretching into the unknown future which will lead us to our true destiny in union with God. He is the Truth, the ultimate Wisdom, on which we can totally rely. He is the Life through whom our faltering life is renewed and made strong and through whom we pass through death to life everlasting. These symbols are not new. They are part of the primeval heritage of the human race. But they have been made new by Christ.

In a passage already quoted Jung referred to the immense power of the Christian symbols over the minds and hearts of the men and women of the Hellenic world of the second century. Why do these symbols not speak with the same force to people today? A religious symbol to be fully effective must belong to two worlds, the world of every day, together with the ideals and aspirations which everyone feels, and the world of the collective unconscious. For the symbol must act as a bridge between these two worlds and therefore needs to have firm foundations in both of them. In the Graeco-Roman world in which Christianity was born the Christian symbols, despite their strangeness, did fit in sufficiently with the ideas and aspirations of the men and women of that day to make a powerful appeal. There were other religions which promised redemption and so prepared people's minds for the gospel.

9 John 14:6

The hunger for spiritual reality and for life after death was nearer the surface of the minds of the men and women of the Hellenic world than it is in our secularized world. The gospel seed fell on ground well prepared, and it had one supreme advantage over its rivals. The Redeemer it proclaimed was not some mythical figure who probably never lived. The gospel announced a Redeemer who had lived and died quite recently, of whose life and teaching, his death and return from the dead there had been many eye-witnesses. You became a Christian by being initiated into membership of a body whose worship was coloured by his memory and his teaching. Through the Christian Church the Christian symbols were bound firmly to the world of every day and so, without any nagging doubts, were able to resound and reverberate powerfully in the inner world of the unconscious.

The situation is very different today. I do not think that the deep needs of mankind have changed appreciably during the past two thousand years, but the symbols which spoke powerfully to those needs in the ancient world have lost much of their power. The cross, the poignant symbol of the unfathomable Godhead reaching down in love to men and women to share their weakness and vulnerability, has become for most people just a Christian badge. For many the Christian symbols have died. Instead of being the best possible expression of an unknown and mysterious reality they have become signs of something known, something which might have been expressed equally well in words, and indeed has been so expressed in a hundred little books of doctrine. For many Jesus Christ is no more than a good man and an inspired teacher who died a long time ago, like Socrates or Marcus Aurelius. The growth of modern science and of science-based technology which has been rapidly changing our way of life has had the effect of concentrating our attention on this world, and the modern idealist is deeply concerned to combat its evils and make it a happier and more comfortable place to live in. The ancient Christian truths seem to have but a shadowy and tenuous reality compared with the overwhelming and omnipresent reality of the world. As was pointed out in an earlier chapter there are many signs today, especially among the young, of a spiritual hunger, of a disillusionment with this world and its values, and of a search for something that this world cannot supply to give meaning to their lives. But the aspirations to which the gospel spoke powerfully in the first days of the Church are buried much deeper in the unconscious of modern men and women than they were with our ancestors two thousand years ago.

If the Christian gospel is to recover its ancient power and the vision of Christ as the Redeemer of twentieth-century men and women is to become compelling there must be a rebirth of symbols. This might be assisted in two ways in particular. First the creative vision of the musician, the artist, the poet and perhaps the choreographer, together with the expertise of the liturgist, will be needed to sharpen and revitalize the old symbols used in worship. In this task the psychology of Jung could provide much help. Second, there is needed a determined effort to relate the Christian symbols to the needs and problems of people today. This will be done most effectively by men and women who have been set on fire by their faith in the Redeemer. The Word, incarnate in Christ, needs to be made visible in the lives of such as Martin Luther King in the USA and Mother Teresa in Calcutta, and in those groups of believers whose shared lives bear persuasive witness to their faith.

6

INDIVIDUATION AND THE ARCHETYPES

In the opening chapters of this book I have presented in outline the more important features of Jung's psychology. In the last chapter I described two archetypes, that of the shadow and that of the deliverer or redeemer and tried to show how they can illuminate our understanding of the Christian gospel and way of life. It is worth while to pause and look back in order to perceive in greater depth the meaning of some of Jung's concepts, especially that of the archetype, and to consider a few other of the archetypes particularly relevant to the theme of this book. We must further look deeper into the part the archetypes play in the process of individuation, that is the process by which an individual is enabled to discover, to acknowledge and to live out his own essential truth. One of the rewards promised by the risen and glorified Christ in the book of Revelation to the individual who is faithful unto death is the gift of a new name which no one knows but the one who receives it. This new personal name can be understood in two ways: as the goal of individuation and as the gift of personal salvation or wholeness.

(i)

Jung put forward the concept of the archetype to account for certain observed facts. The human infant, like the offspring of other animals, responds to some stimuli and not to others. Not only psychologists are aware of this fact; every parent has noted it too. Jung was concerned to understand the psychic principle behind this selectivity of response. He called the choosing principle the archetype. By it he understood an inherited tendency, closely allied to instinct, which is aroused by certain images. The archetype is asleep until the appropriate image awakens it. The archetype of the shadow, referred to in the last chapter, lies dormant until it is triggered awake by the image of a disagreeable figure representing some rejected element of the personality, whether personified in a dream or projected on to a real-life person. Similarly the deliverer or saviour archetype is roused, especially in times of crisis, by someone possessed of outstanding qualities of leadership.

The archetype of the shadow, of evil, and the archetype of the saviour are primordial; they go back to the origins of mankind hundreds of thousands of years before Christ. Many a great tribal or national leader has been able to unite men and women in the face of some natural disaster or under threat from human enemies, because he was able to arouse this instinctive, archetypal response. Jesus Christ awakened in some of his contemporaries this primeval response as one who could liberate men and women from moral and spiritual evil. But if we can see Christ as standing in a long line of great human leaders we must also see him as uniquely different. Some of that difference was described in the last chapter.

For if Jesus Christ awakens in people the deep, instinctive tendency to turn in their spiritual trouble to one who will save them, the saviour archetype, he also stirs into activity a deeper tendency still, the archetype of the self. Let us look further at the idea of the self, already referred to in Chapter 3 and central to the theme of this book. Jung saw the self both as representing the total personality which, as it were, presses and persuades the individual to live out more and more of what he truly is, and also as representing God. This psychological concept of the self resembles in some respects the theological idea of God's image in man. This idea was expounded in this way by St Irenaeus, a bishop in Gaul at the end of the second century AD. Basing himself on the

sentence in the book of Genesis which describes God as cre-
ating man in his own image and likeness,[1] he takes image and
likeness to refer to different but related realities. The image
of God denotes a certain God-like character in man, especially
his intelligence and free will, which distinguishes him from
the lower animals and which he cannot lose without ceasing
to be human. The likeness of God is something more; it is a
moral and spiritual resemblance to God which we have lost
through the Fall and the consequent estrangement from God,
from our fellows and from our own true nature, which is
called original sin. To see the likeness of God we must look
not at the men and women of our acquaintance but at Jesus
Christ. The Christian life can be understood as the progres-
sive restoration of the lost likeness. Theology, then, turning
to reflect on psychology will see the individuation process as
a natural development which grace assists and perfects. As
more and more we are able to accept and express in our lives
the hitherto rejected or unacknowledged elements of our
being, we increasingly realize ourselves, we recover the divine
likeness. The psychological fact that our own nature presses
us to realize ourselves as much as possible, and leaves us
discontented in so far as we fail to do so, answers the theological maxim that we are created, each in his own individual
way, to correspond with the divine likeness.

(ii)

We must turn now to consider one of those sayings of Jung
which the Christian at first hearing is likely to find disconcerting. He speaks of Christ as a symbol of the self. The
saying becomes more acceptable if we bear in mind that for
Jung the self, the total personality with its unknown heights
and depths, that sometimes addresses the individual in tones
of absolute authority, is a symbol of God himself. It is because
in Christian experience Christ speaks with absolute authority
that Jung can call him a symbol of the self. He is using the
language of psychology which is concerned with how reality

1 Gen. 1:26

is experienced rather than what it is. Speaking as a psychologist Jung is affirming that Christ is experienced as divine. Whether he is in fact divine is not something on which as a psychologist he can pronounce.

But there is a further disconcerting fact which needs to be faced. Jung did not regard the Christ of Christian devotion as a wholly satisfactory symbol of the self. His reason for this was that at any rate in the Christian imagination Christ is a figure wholly light, containing no darkness. He cannot therefore stand for the darker aspects of human nature. Jung is here concerned with what is *felt* to be evil because it seems to be a threat to what is felt to be good. The dark aspects of human nature are not in fact evil and would become good if they could be accepted by the conscious individual and integrated with the rest of his personality. This, though theoretically possible, cannot in practice be fully achieved. Jung thought that the idealized Christ of Christian devotion, by repressing the darker side of human nature, made this approximation more difficult and hindered the individual from accepting and living out what he truly is.

Before attempting to answer this criticism that Jung makes I believe we have to acknowledge much truth in it. It is possible for a Christian to have so false or inadequate a conception of Christ as to damage his relationship with God and hinder the action of grace. It is normal, as was pointed out in the last chapter, for the individual in his battle with his unruly impulses and emotions to form an ideal which contradicts them and helps to keep them under. It is natural that the ideal thus formed by the Christian should fuse with his idea of Christ. Indeed it is all too easy for me to fashion Christ in the image of my ideal, to dwell on the qualities which I find attractive or inspiring and to ignore the rest. If for example I have a problem in controlling my anger which is apt to explode uncontrollably, hurting other people and making me feared and disliked, I may without fully realizing what I am doing, use Christ, or my image of Christ, to keep under my anger. I am likely to dwell on his gentle qualities, his compassion for the sick and the sinful and his love of children and forget his sterner characteristics, his anger as he overturned the tables of the money-changers in the temple or denounced the hypocrisy of some of the scribes and Pharisees. And though my devotion to a one-sided image of Christ may help me to contain my anger, it could, unless my picture of Christ is enlarged, hinder the growth of such qualities as courage and fortitude which draw some of their strength from anger under control.

One remedy for a too-narrow image of Christ is to reflect on the total picture of Christ as presented in the Gospels. But there are problems here which must be acknowledged. One of these is that we read the Gospels through twentieth-century spectacles and perceive only what the presuppositions of our time permit us to see. The work of New Testament scholars helps us to shed some of the false presuppositions and to get nearer to the actual historical Jesus, who is now recognized to be very much a man of his times, a Jew steeped in the traditions of his people. It is impossible for us to recapture fully the likeness and character of the historic Jesus of Nazareth. But even if we could there would be a further problem for the Christian who believes that God himself addresses us in that human figure. For the whole Godhead could not conceivably be disclosed in the thirty years of the life of a man belonging to a particular race and culture and living at a particular point in time. The New Testament however indicates a solution of the problem. For the Christ of Christian faith is indeed the same Jesus who walked and taught in Palestine, but a Jesus transformed by his dying and rising again and his life in unclouded union with the Father. For St Paul Christ is a heavenly figure,[2] in the book of Revelation he is described as a man arrayed in the symbols of Godhead.[3] In St John's gospel he is the Word through whom all things were made and the light of all men everywhere.[4] The Christ who is the object of Christian worship is both the Jesus who lived and died in Palestine and a much greater, in the kind of way that a full-grown man is greater than the young child he once was. If our worship were concentrated solely upon the historical Jesus it would leave small room for art or science in

2   1 Cor. 15:45–49
3   Rev. 1:12–20
4   John 1:1, 5, 9

which so far as the records go he showed no interest. Further his prophetic and more than prophetic vocation involved a narrowing of interest, a concentration upon what is essential in our approach to God. He taught and embodied a way of salvation and is silent about a hundred thousand matters of concern to us today. Even in the sphere of religion he says nothing about the insights of Hinduism or Buddhism. The Christ as the Gospels and the rest of the New Testament describe him is the indispensable clue to the Christ who is the centre of our worship. Yet Christ shares in the unfathomable reality of the Godhead. He is the Unknown and the best pictures we can form of him are no more than pointers to one vastly greater than we can imagine. Jung's criticism is a salutary warning of the effects of a narrow or sentimental devotion to Christ; but it is not valid against a deeper, indeed a more traditional, understanding of Christ as the divine Word through whom the universe came into being.

This excursion into the much debated territory of Christology has been undertaken in order to show that the concept of the self and of individuation need not conflict with the Christian faith in Christ as divine. But we must now turn to consider some of the other archetypes which have a special bearing on the process of individuation. After the confrontation with the shadow and the assimilation so far as possible of what is positive in it an individual next needs to come to terms with the contrasexual elements of his personality. Every man has feminine elements in him, every woman has masculine elements in her. In some individuals the characteristics of the opposite sex are small, in others they are almost as great as those of his own sex. In the course of growing up a boy rejects as far as he can his girlish tendencies; he plays boys' games and follows boys' interests. Similarly girls are discouraged from the roughness and rowdiness which is expected of boys. They play with dolls up to an age when a boy would not dare to be seen with one. The whole of our education, both at home and at school, encourages a boy to behave like a boy and to grow up into a man and equally the girl to develop her feminine characteristics and not to be a tomboy. In this we are following deep-seated racial tendencies which go back presumably to the beginning of the human race. For the sexes are complementary; man needs woman and woman needs man. If we tried to teach boys and girls so far as possible to be unisex and interchangeable, this would be detrimental to the race in which from time immemorial men and women have formed partnerships in which each helped to make good the weaknesses and defects of the other. This is not contradicted by the fact that the actual roles that women play are by no means wholly determined by the woman's biological function of child-bearing and are largely influenced by the changing expectations imposed on them by society.

This developing of the individual in accordance with the ideal proper to his sex is a task which belongs to the first half of life. When by recognizing and accepting the positive elements in his shadow side he has become sufficiently mature it is important for him or her to come to terms with those elements of the other sex that have perforce been kept under. Jung calls this contrasexual element in man the anima and in woman the animus. The normal way in which the individual comes to realize the power of the archetype of the other sex is through falling in love. When Jack falls in love with Jill the image of Jill awakens the undeveloped feminine in Jack. Through falling in love Jack sees in Jill, without understanding it, a hitherto unknown aspect of himself. No wonder that he feels a kind of enchantment. The image of Jill makes him feel more himself, more alive, more at peace. At least this is so if Jill responds to his adoration sympathetically; if not Jack will be in misery. It is as though his life and happiness depend on Jill's acceptance of him. So long as the enchantment lasts he is emotionally tied to her and dependent on her. For what he sees in her is his own feminine side, his anima, part of himself, projected onto her. No doubt there is something in Jill which makes her a suitable recipient of his projection rather than her sister Jennie whom many think more attractive. As everyone knows the bitter-sweet enchantment of being in love does not last. If Jill is in love with Jack she will see in him the personification of her own masculine side, her animus in Jung's terminology. Perhaps the two decide to get married. In that case the fierce explosion of being in love may well give way to the steady flame of an affectionate caring love which will carry them through the hazards and pitfalls of marriage. For sooner or later the projections will be withdrawn and they will come to see each other more truly as they are. They can grow to love each other more genuinely. Before they were in love with an idealized aspect of the other; afterwards they can love the real person that each is, with all the tiresome defects and minor incompatibilities.

The biological and social ends of marriage, the procreation of children and their care and nurture in a warm and stable environment, are not the only though they are of course the primary ends of marriage. Marriage, or at least some close friendship with one or more of the opposite sex, is nature's way of encouraging men and women to come to terms with the contrasexual elements of their own being. In other words it can be a step in the process of individuation, a rung on the ladder of self-awareness. This function of marriage as a help in the process of individuation is closely woven into its biological function. Neither marriage nor deep friendship with the opposite sex is in all cases essential to individuation, though perhaps some kind of real friendship is. For it is possible for some, at any rate, to learn to recognize and accept the other side of themselves by a deliberately cultivated introspection into and searching of their own depths. Meditation, contemplation and the disciplines of the spiritual life can also foster a profound self-awareness. Nevertheless some deep and intimate friendship is highly desirable and for most people essential, for the reason that it is very difficult to accept ourselves with all our defects and weaknesses unless others or at least one other accept us. We need the reassurance which can only be given by someone who both knows us intimately and accepts us as we are, if we are to accept ourselves fully.

The mysterious psychic realities termed by Jung the anima and animus are often contaminated by and confused with the unfaced personal shadow, the rejected and despised elements of the personality. As we have seen, a man's personal shadow represents rejected elements of his masculine potential, his capacity to fight, for example. In that case he might be haunted in his dreams by a thug who is out to murder him. This unfaced part of him might very likely fuse with the anima, the unfaced feminine in him, which would then become a destructive force within his personality. A common form of the anima in its negative aspect is that of the possessive mother who prevents her children from growing up and living their lives independently of her. In the language of dream and mythology the anima in its destructive aspect appears as a dragon whom the hero must kill if he is to fulfil his quest. Thus in the modern myth, *The Lord of the Rings*, Frodo with his companion, Samwise, on their journey to the evil land of Mordor to fulfil the task laid upon Frodo, are led by Gollum, Frodo's treacherous shadow, into the dark cave passages where lurks Shelob, the giant spider with evil intelligence and deadly bite. It is only after a hair-raising but eventually successful battle with the monster that the two companions are able to go forward on their dangerous mission.

It is partly because of the threatening aspect of the contrasexual in us that it is of essential importance at the very outset of the road to individuation to have recognized and come to terms with our weak and faulty side. Of course the monster, the devouring mother, corresponds to a tendency in ourselves. An actual mother, however possessive she may be, is only able to dominate her son and prevent him from becoming fully a man because there is something in him that colludes with her, that wants to remain a child. There is something in us that prefers to be looked after and protected, rather than face the risks of fighting our own battles. It may be said that this is a fanciful and highly coloured way of describing a fairly common occurrence, that of the possessive mother and the over-dependent son. But the ties which bind mother and son in this unhealthy relationship are deeply rooted in the unconscious and can be extremely hard to sever. And in the effort to break away into freedom the mythical picture of the hero fighting the dragon can reverberate powerfully in the unconscious and can help to release the fighting determination which the young man will need if he is to stop depending on his mother and grow up.

It is not only or principally in its negative aspect of the devouring dragon, who must be fought and overcome, that the anima appears in the dreams of individuals and in the mythologies of mankind. In *The Lord of the Rings* Galadriel personifies the anima in its helpful aspect. She gives Frodo a magic phial which shines in darkness and strikes fear into the hearts of creatures of the dark. Only with the help of Galadriel's gift is the monstrous Shelob overcome. The feminine in a man, if he can learn to rely on it without identifying with it, can give him an inner wisdom, sympathy and strength. A woman has a similar task on the journey to individuation of coming to terms with her own masculine side, her animus; she needs to learn how to rely on these masculine elements without identifying with them. The woman who identifies with her animus and allows it to dominate tends to be argumentative and unyielding in her assertion of views which she has not thought out but has gained at second hand. A man, on the other hand, who identifies with his anima tends to be effeminate and sentimental.

(iii)

There are other important archetypes to be considered. The theologian will see these inherited instinctive tendencies as part of the way in which the Creator immanent in each of his creatures guides, persuades and warns the individual with a view to his realizing to the fullest possible extent his innate capacities. Each person in the process of becoming fully himself has to recognize and face up to the unknown energies stirring within him as well as the forces which confront him from outside. Jung by naming and personifying the archetypes provides us with images which can help us to perceive and reckon with the mysterious and powerful tendencies they represent. The believer who sees God at work in these archetypal tendencies will understand his coming to terms with them as part of his commitment to God and his following of Christ. No doubt the great majority of those who seek to commit themselves to God and his Kingdom do so without any knowledge of Jung or of his theory of archetypes and of individuation. The inner tendencies which his theories try to explain do operate, however little we may understand it, and many people are more or less blindly following the path of individuation partly by trusting their intuition, partly by learning from mistakes, partly with the help of traditional wisdom embodying the experience of the past. What Jung's theory of archetypes can do is to bring some clarity into our understanding of what is taking place within us, and so enable us to co-operate better with the forces of growth as well as to avoid some of the pitfalls of the spiritual journey. Let us then consider a few more of the archetypes of special importance on the road to individuation.

There is the archetype of the old wise man, the embodiment of spirit, which is important particularly in the development of men. It resembles the father archetype, but is more a kind of racial father, the embodiment of the wisdom of the race. An ancestral wisdom, a capacity for vision, for seeing into the meaning of things and of divining the course of the future can help a man to fulfil responsibility as a leader and guide to his fellows. Many who have achieved a position of great responsibility have found themselves supported by an inner wisdom greater than anything that their personal experience could have accounted for. An individual thus inwardly enlightened needs to realize that this wisdom is not his own personal possession, it is something entrusted to him as to a steward, it is a kind of grace. If he identifies with it as though it was his own personal wisdom his individuality will be diminished. He is likely to become doctrinaire; all his other interests are liable to be swallowed up in some great idea or cause; his family and friends may come to seem mere adjuncts to the idea that has gripped him rather than persons in their own right. He is likely to lose his sense of humour. Our first experience of the power of this archetype is usually through projecting it on to some outstanding figure who will then seem to embody all wisdom. Jung himself must have been seen by many as the universal sage. His personality and ideas were such as to awaken in his disciples this archetypal tendency. I can myself recall a phase through which I passed when I was inclined to accept all Jung's ideas uncritically as the final word of wisdom – which of course was the very last thing that Jung himself would have wished. This tendency to reach out to and rely on a wisdom greater than one's own personal wisdom is what Jung means by the archetype of the old wise man. It is as though there lived in the depths of the personality a sage or seer to whom one might turn in times of perplexity. Such a figure sometimes appears in dreams as one endowed with great authority and conveys better than any abstract statement the reality of this inner wisdom.

Another archetype especially important in the individuation process of women is that of the great mother. It is the symbol of feminine wisdom and compassion. Every child whatever his sex is inevitably dependent on his mother. For nine months the infant grows in his mother's womb and for two or three years after birth is normally surrounded by the psychic atmosphere of his mother. When the mother is able to fulfil her maternal task sufficiently well the child will be likely to grow up contentedly and at the appropriate time break free from his mother's influence in order to follow his own path through life. When the mother is unable to fulfil her task satisfactorily the archetype of the racial mother is likely to be activated and the child will crave for an ideal mother who can give what the actual mother failed to supply. The great mother archetype is of an all-accepting, all-understanding, all-forgiving being whose love and protection the deprived child craves for. A person so handicapped may grow up, and indeed go through life, hopelessly searching for someone who will play towards him the role of the all-accepting mother. A woman needs to take care not to identify with the archetype and see herself as all-loving, all-understanding. If she falls into this mistake she will want to mother everyone and will be utterly miserable if she has no one to take care of. In fact she is likely to do much harm by trying to take care of people who do not need or want to be taken care of. A person who sees herself as the all-accepting, all-understanding mother could be experienced by those dependent on her as the destructive, all-devouring mother. On the other hand the great mother archetype is an inner potential, which, recognized to be a gift or grace and not a personal possession, has enabled women to be true mothers to people in need. The great mother archetype like that of the old wise man is an aspect of the self and so carries with it sometimes an atmosphere of the numinous and something of the authority of the divine.

(*iv*)

I mention two other archetypes of especial significance in the process of individuation. There is first the archetype of the child, boy or girl, the symbol of hidden potential, of the possibility of marvellous growth and therefore the symbol of hope. There are many ancient legends and myths of the mysterious birth of a wonderful child who grows up to be a hero or great leader. In these stories the child is usually exposed to great hazards after birth but, weak and helpless, is strangely protected and enabled to grow up to fulfil his mission. There is the well-known Greek story of the birth of Heracles and the even better-known story of the birth of Moses and his exposure in a tiny ark placed in the bulrushes which fringe the Nile. This archetype lies behind the prophecy of Isaiah: 'Unto us a child is born, unto us a son is given; and the governmen will be upon his shoulder, and his name will be called Wonderful Counsellor, Mighty God, Everlasting Father, Prince of Peace.'[5] Best known of all to Christians is the New Testament story of the birth of the Christ child, the threat to his life at the hands of Herod's soldiers and his escape into Egypt.

In the course of life a man or woman often reaches an apparent dead end. Like Dante, lost in a dark wood, the individual feels that his old aims and pursuits have lost their interest, life has become stale. At such a juncture the symbol of the child, appearing in a dream or waking fantasy or projected on to an actual child, can become the powerful sign of new possibilities. The child symbol points to a potential child in us, to the possibility of renouncing the old stale outlook, of making a fresh beginning, of becoming in spirit like a child, vulnerable like a child, but like a child sponta- neous and open to new ways. The archetype brings home to us that we cannot save ourselves by our own skill and deter- mination; we must be, as it were, born again, a new attitude must be allowed to grow in us. Like other archetypes there is an ambiguity about that of the child. Just as the mother can stand both as the symbol of the beneficent mother and of

5 Isa. 9:6

the possessive, devouring mother, so the symbol of the child can stand both for a quality of childlikeness which is only possible to a mature adult, and the childishness which apes it and, until it is renounced, hinders growth to full maturity. The child archetype represents an innate possibility which the appropriate circumstances call into activity. As with the other archetypes it is important not to identify with this archetype. The man who does so becomes the perpetual boy, the Peter Pan, whose fellows cannot take him seriously, because he never grows up but clings to the irresponsibility of childhood.

The second of the two archetypes is that of the treasure, hard to find and dangerous to look for. It is sometimes seen as the diamond, the point of light, the jewel in the lotus. This, like the child archetype in one of its meanings, is a symbol of the self, of the total personality of the individual and also the central core of his being. The mythologies are full of stories of a quest fraught with danger in search of a treasure beyond price. Sometimes the treasure is hidden in a cave guarded by a serpent or dragon; sometimes it is sunk in water, a symbol of the unconscious. The real quest is an inner one and involves facing the hazards of the unconscious. In the well-known Greek myth of the golden fleece, the object of the quest of Jason and his companions in the Argonaut was guarded by a serpent. The world's literature, from the many accounts of the Quest of the Holy Grail to Stevenson's *Treasure Island*, testifies to the perennial fascination of stories about the search for treasure. But the true goal of this archetype is a spiritual one. Misunderstood, this deep archetypal urge can lead a person to make becoming a millionaire the great aim of his life. But whoever sacrifices everything in order to become rich will find that he has thwarted and stunted his own being. 'What shall it profit a man if he should gain the whole world and lose his own soul?'[6] The treasure, the pearl of great price, for which a person must be prepared to sacrifice everything that he has is, in psychological terms, his self-realization or individuation; in theological terms it is salvation. We cannot

6   Mark 8:36

help wanting this once we have become aware of it as a possibility. The quest is the search for individuation.

This brief and over-simplified account of a few of the archetypes conveys no idea of the number, wealth and variety of the archetypal themes which Jung discovered in the dreams of his patients and the myths, fairy stories and legends of all races. The importance of Jung's researches into ancient religion and myth is that they shed light on the structure and development of the human psyche. In trying to understand Jung's ideas it is necessary to bear in mind his affirmation that the symbol is the best expression available of an unknown reality. It is important not to explain away the symbol as merely the pictorial expression of a well-known fact – as someone might explain the Oedipus story as just an illustration of the well-known fact that sons do often grow up to be the rivals of their fathers for the love of their mothers. But it is even more important to relate the archetypal symbols to real-life situations in the present and not to regard them as one might a romantic novel, as an opportunity of entering a world of fantasy. What is needed is a kind of dialogue between the practical workaday self, the ego, and the unconscious, incurably romantic in its style of expression but bearing within it the experience of the race.

Part of the discipline of the Christian's spiritual life is designed to bring the insights and the inspiration of the inner life to bear on his conduct in the outer life, in his relations with his fellows and his responsibilities towards his family and his country. In the next and final chapter we shall examine the light Jung's teaching can shed on the practices of the spiritual life.

7

INDIVIDUATION AND THE SPIRITUAL LIFE

(i)

In this final chapter I hope to draw together some of the hints and suggestions of the previous chapters about the bearing of Jung's theories upon the Christian life, and to add further reflections more especially about its bearing on prayer. It might be thought that Jung who did not regard faith in God as important would have little to contribute to the practice of prayer, which is an expression of faith. But the reason why Jung undervalued belief in God was the immense store he set on the experience of God – 'I don't need to believe, I know'. I think Jung was mistaken in so exalting the value of his experience of God as to overlook the importance of belief, but not more so than many Christian teachers who have stressed the importance of blind faith and disregarded experience as of only minor significance. For in truth both belief and experience have their necessary place in a mature faith. 'I know whom I have believed,' writes St Paul.[1] It is in this area of experience or intuitive knowledge that Jung can help the modern Christian. For some of the pillars that supported the faith of his grandparents have been seriously shaken if not

1   2 Tim. 1:12

destroyed. In our pluralist society the Christian no longer has the support of knowing that most people, at least in a general way, share his faith. The authority of the Bible has been weakened both by the biblical critics and by the scientific world view very different from the biblical picture of the cosmos. Nor is the authority of the Church any longer strong enough to reassure the doubter. In this situation many are searching for an experience that will partly at least make up for the shaking of the old pillars of faith. In this search Jung can do much to help.

I think that Jung can help us to experience, to know, the God whom we believe in. But I must confess my conviction that a firm belief in God such as Jung did not permit himself to hold (though he did admit to believing in God's existence) is essential for the fullest kind of prayer. For if we are right to commit ourselves to this belief certain consequences follow. Prayer has much more to do with God's search for us than our search for him. We could not have any knowledge of our Creator unless he chose to disclose himself to us. Our prayer is a response to God's prior initiative. God makes himself known by innumerable signs which those who have ears to hear and eyes to see recognize as from him. Some of the signs are in the world outside the individual, some of them are within him. Jung's individuation process describes part of the divine strategy by means of which he leads men and women both to become aware of him and to realize their potential to the full as they learn more and more to trust themselves to him. The phases, the difficulties, the struggles of the individuation process can be seen by the believer as the pressure of the presence of the unseen God, union with whom spells freedom and fulfilment. As a Christian I believe that these inner signs need to be complemented by outward signs and especially by the worship, fellowship and sacraments of the contemporary Church, the community of believers, who bear witness to the unique self-disclosure of God in Jesus Christ and to Christ's living presence with them. Jung's special wisdom is his power to illuminate the inner signs. He can, I believe, help the Christian to recognize and respond to God's presence within his own experience. I propose then to look at the practice of prayer in the light of Jung's teaching about the individuation process, to see how far each can illuminate the other.

(ii)

Jung's teaching about the stages of life has direct relevance to Christian prayer. For there is a prayer suitable to life's morning and another more suitable to the afternoon and evening. It is easy to make the mistake of trying to carry into the second half of life a style of prayer that suited well in the first half and in consequence to be thoroughly discouraged. It would be an equal though less likely mistake to try in the morning to pray in a manner that belongs to the afternoon. In youth, when it is important to break away from dependence on one's parents and to establish oneself in the adult world, the individual rightly seeks from God the courage and skill to do this. Jung will teach him to see this courage and skill as flowing from within him. He will try to put aside his fears and rely on God to activate whatever innate talents he has. In the second half of life he normally needs to loosen his hold on the ambitions that spurred him on earlier and allow another side of himself, perforce starved or repressed earlier, to come to the fore. His prayer will tend to be more contemplative, more a waiting on God, which will allow his neglected side to rise into consciousness and enrich and deepen him. There will be many exceptions to this rough rule but the principles underlying it, I believe, are sound.

Jung was very conscious of the mysteriousness of the human personality and the difficulty of penetrating the outward appearance and discovering the real individual. It was partly to bring some order into the diversity of actual people that he devised his theory of human types which was touched on in Chapter 4. His analysis is of course incomplete, but for all its limitations it offers a useful set of conceptual tools for trying to explore the differences between human beings. The tools are not easy to apply in particular cases. It is not easy as a rule for an individual to be sure to which type he himself belongs, let alone other people. The reason for the difficulty is that I am aware of adopting both introvert and extravert attitudes at different times; and if I turn to the four functions – sensation, thinking, feeling and intuition – I am equally aware of using all the four functions but am usually not clear which of them I rely on most. For this reason, in applying these insights to prayer it is desirable to experiment to discover the right way of prayer for myself. It is probably best for an individual to begin with a kind of prayer that gives scope to his most developed functions. If I am a person of thinking type some kind of discursive or reflective meditation may be the best way into the attitude of prayer. If feeling is my strong function then I shall enter into prayer best by expressing gratitude, penitence, trust or love in my prayer. The individual of sensation type will profit by using the body to express his worship and trust. The intuitive type will probably be drawn to a contemplative waiting on God. But, however we may begin, sooner or later it will be important to enlist all the functions in our approach to God.[2]

The ancient practice of *lectio divina*, spiritual reading, can be made a valuable instrument for involving the whole personality in responding to God. This reading, quite unlike most secular reading, is, properly understood, a kind of meditation, a means of communing both with God and with one's own depths. It is, I think, important that we should use this reading to develop, if we can, our weaker or less developed functions. Thus, if I am a thinker I must do what I can to allow my feelings to be roused, to express judgements of value, of right and wrong. If I am of feeling type I must not skate over a thought-provoking passage but must make myself reflect on it, perhaps by writing down some comment on it or summary of the argument. One should pause over a passage that strikes home and causes reverberations deep within and not resume reading until the words or ideas have made their full impact. Sometimes when a passage seems utterly flat and boring it is well to pause. It may be that the boredom is due to an inner resistance to what the passage is saying. At such times it may be well to ask myself, 'Why am I unwilling to listen to what this author is saying to me? Is it perhaps too

2   See my 'Prayer and Different Types of People' in *The Heart in Pilgrimage* (Seabury 1980), Appendix

near the bone? Is it perhaps trying to teach me something
that I don't want to know?' Reading done in this way is a
means to that interaction between consciousness and the unconscious which Jung encouraged in his patients. It is possible
to look upon this kind of reflective reading as a means of
fostering the individuation process, as it enlarges my consciousness by allowing into it more and more of what has
been unconscious. But it would be equally true to see it as a
means of responding to God as he leads me to become more
aware of his presence within me, as he invites me into closer
union with himself.

This kind of reading can be seen both as a prelude to
prayer and as a means of enlarging self-awareness. The teaching of Jung would lead us to look out for and take careful note
of the symbols and images that awaken echoes within. Jung
is not unique among psychologists in stressing the importance
of self-awareness; all the schools of dynamic psychology encourage it. Jung's especial contribution to our self-under-
standing lies in his personification of the inner forces of the
psyche, or rather his naming them after the images under
which they appear in the dreams, myths and fairy-tales of the
human race. In the quest for self-knowledge it is a great help
to be able to identify the strange forces at work within us and
to give them a name. Jung provides us with a set of names
which enable us in part to understand these energies and
confront them. In ancient times it was believed that if you
could correctly name a demon you could exercise power over
it. In modern medicine an accurate diagnosis is the first step
to prescribing suitable treatment. But the sicknesses of the
psyche are more like the interference of demons than a virus
infection. And the health of the soul depends on achieving a
right relation with these forces. For understood sufficiently
and faced rightly they act like guardian angels, whereas misunderstood, feared and thwarted they may assume the character of destructive demons.

One of Jung's key principles for lighting up the workings
of the human psyche is the compensatory function of the
unconscious, which is ceaselessly pressing to balance and
correct the one-sidedness of the conscious person. This sheds
light on the tension between the spirit and the flesh, familiar

to those committed to the Christian way, which resembles the tension between intuition and sensation. The effort to realize the presence of the unseen Godhead leads the individual to try to disregard the solicitations of the senses, especially those of sight and hearing. I enter my inner sanctuary, when I pray, and shut the door on distractions from without. But the senses cannot be so treated with impunity. They will tend to counteract, either by making concentration impossible by their continual interruptions with irrelevant trains of thought or fantasies, or, if I am determined enough to exclude them while I am actually praying, they will cause a violent reaction afterwards in an obsessive desire for food and drink, the explosion of physical sex, or intense feelings of irritability or resentment. If with the help of a strong ideal and a determined will I am able to suppress these reactions then a mood of depression, of soul-weariness usually sets in. This was well known to old spiritual writers under the name of accidie. One of the old methods of dealing with this reaction by the body was severe physical asceticism, such as fasting, self-flagellation or standing naked in icy water. It is doubtful if this method is of value today, except for the small minority of individuals whose senses are exceptionally vigorous. A much more effective way, at least for most people, of dealing with the body is to treat it not as an enemy to be crushed but as a potential friend and ally. Many Christians of the West are learning valuable lessons from eastern systems of spirituality, Hindu and Buddhist, in how to bring the body into harmony with the soul. The physical exercises of yoga are designed so that, relaxed and contented, the body leaves the mind free to concentrate. A number of books by Christian writers have made simple adaptations of eastern methods for the use of Christians.[3] Deep breathing, breath control and learning to attend to the breath as it enters and leaves the lungs, and the cultivation of an awareness of the sensations of the body are an important element in this eastern teaching. It is sometimes

3   Déchanet, *Christian Yoga* (Burns, Oates 1960); Antony de Mello, *Sadhana* (Seabury Press 1984); William Johnston, *The Mirror Mind* (Harper & Row 1981)

thought that this cultivation of body-awareness is in some way unhealthy and is likely to lead to bodily self-indulgence; but in truth the opposite is the case. The repression of bodily feeling is unhealthy. Only as we become aware of the body, its feelings and its urges, are we able to control it. Repressed or ignored it falls out of control. Further, awareness of the body's sensations is part of the self-awareness which is the road to the awareness of God.

(iii)

The value of Jung's teaching for the practice of prayer can best be demonstrated by allowing it to illuminate the traditional fourfold division of prayer into the four acts or attitudes of adoration, confession, thanksgiving and petition. From the psychological point of view adoration or worship means the acknowledgement of supreme or absolute value. Jung believes that there is a God archetype, that is an inherited tendency, latent in all people – it might almost be termed a God instinct – awaiting a suitable object to summon it into activity. Failing the right object it may be aroused by some substitute cause or goal, whether individual, such as success or fame, or social, such as one's country. It is this God archetype, or absolutist tendency, that leads people to give altogether exaggerated value to objects of real but limited worth, thus making little gods or idols of them. The prayer of adoration directs the individual to give supreme value to God, the Creator and Author of all genuine human values. The Christian Church's public worship is designed both to arouse the God-instinct and to accord absolute value and authority to God as disclosed in Jesus Christ. The powerful symbolism of the Eucharist makes it the most efficacious means of involving men and women deeply in adoration.[4]

Jung's linking of the God archetype with that of the self, so that it is not always possible to distinguish the one from the other, reinforces the Christian doctrine of God's immanence

4   See Jung, *Transformation Symbolism in the Mass. C.W.*, vol. xi. Also ch. 10 of my *Heart in Pilgrimage*

within the creation and in men and women. Nor need the equally important doctrine of the divine transcendence which balances the truth of his immanence in any way clash with Jung's teaching. For Jung regards the experience of God both as something felt within the soul and also as being an experience of absolute authority. It is to be feared that many have been brought up to conceive of God as a Being wholly external to themselves without any idea of his immanence within them. Such an externalized idea of God would inevitably, it would seem, whether or not he was thought of as all-loving and all-wise, make the development of an individual's full humanity more difficult. To worship God as one intimately within us, though immensely transcending our intellect's grasp, is to anchor us securely and give us a sense of stability, thus enabling us to affirm ourselves without arrogance and to love and serve others without pretence or servility. Or rather, our worship will tend to foster these attitudes in us in proportion to its genuineness. Many of Jung's religionless patients after prolonged analysis were led to this attitude of profound reverence and found a meaning to life and a cure of their neurosis in their change of outlook. This attitude of reverence and acceptance towards reality achieved by analysis is what adoration rightly understood encourages.

Adoration, the ascription of absolute authority to the divine Reality, both within and around yet at the same time infinitely above us, is the most fundamental of all the modes of prayer. Without some tincture of it the other acts and attitudes by which we acknowledge God are seriously defective. Indeed the other kinds of prayer can be understood as aspects of adoration, adoration expressed in a particular context. The prayer of confession can be seen as adoration articulated in the context of evil and sin. Jung's teaching can be of especial help to Christians in this area. For he insists on the human value of facing and acknowledging not only our actual shortcomings and sins but their roots in the unconscious so far as we are able to unearth them. What he writes about neurosis is highly relevant here, for neurosis approximates very closely to what the Christian means by temptation. Like neurosis temptation is involuntary, it happens to me. A neurosis is a constellation of repressed emotions and desires which interferes with our conscious intentions and actions. Although a mild neurosis is a nuisance and embarrassment and a severe one can be crippling, yet neuroses are an invaluable source of self-knowledge. Jung writes:

> We should not try to 'get rid' of a neurosis, but rather experience what it means, what it has to teach, what its purpose is. We should even learn to be thankful for it, otherwise we pass it by and miss the opportunity of getting to know ourselves as we really are. A neurosis is only truly removed when it has removed the false attitude of the ego. We do not cure it, it cures us. A man is ill, but the illness is nature's attempt to heal him. From the illness we can learn so much for our recovery, and what the neurotic flings away as absolutely worthless contains the true gold we should never have found elsewhere.[5]

Here is advice from which the Christian can profit as he struggles with his inner trials, for these are the effect of a kind of neurosis. Though perhaps provoked by persons or happenings external to us they arise from the unconscious. By bringing home to us what manner of people we are and what explosive emotions and urges are concealed in our depths they can bring about a change in our conscious attitude, the *metanoia* to which the gospel summons us.

The subject of sin and guilt is apt to set the modern Christian pastor or writer somewhat on edge because he has been made thoroughly aware of the damaging effects of a sense of guilt on a great many men and women today, some of them in mental homes. In common with all psychologists Jung was fully aware of what can only be called the sickness of a morbid guilt which is out of all proportion to any actual misdeeds. But, swimming against the stream as usual, he was more concerned to stress the reality of a corporate guilt in which all mankind is involved as a psychic reality, and the human value of acknowledging guilt.

> If only people could realize what an enrichment it is to find one's own guilt, what a sense of honour and spiritual dig-

nity! But nowhere does there seem a glimmering of this insight. Instead we hear only of attempts to shift the blame on to others.[6]

Jung comments wryly on the post-war confession by the Christian leaders of Germany of their share in the guilt of Germany for the war and the atrocities which accompanied it. They spoilt the whole effect of their confession of guilt by going on to point out that other nations besides Germany were to blame, which, true though it was, was something for others, not themselves, to acknowledge. Jung regarded the whole of Germany to be guilty of the crimes committed under the leadership of Hitler, despite the honourable minority who opposed his regime. Indeed he regarded the whole of Europe, including his own neutral Switzerland, as sharing in the guilt of Hitler's war crimes. Mankind in his view carries a burden of collective guilt. This can be seen as due to an archetypal tendency to feel guilt at the failure to act up to the standard of true humanity, which corresponds to what theologians know as original sin. If only we can freely acknowledge our falling short and not attempt either to justify ourselves or to blame others we can live at peace. This sheds light on the teaching of Jesus that if we are to be forgiven we must forgive – and forgive from the heart; and also on the petition in the Lord's prayer, 'Forgive us our sins as we forgive those who sin against us'. It may be that the epidemic of morbid guilt mentioned earlier is directly related to the fact that most people repress their guilt feelings instead of acknowledging their guilt. Those weighed down by morbid guilt feelings are perhaps bearing the burden of the unacknowledged guilt of their self-satisfied fellows.

In confession the believer turns to God who is active in the centre of his being. In addressing God he is at the same time entering into a kind of dialogue with the self, with his unknown depths where God is at work, and so is fostering the healthy interaction of his conscious personality with the unconscious. He will see confession as among other things the declaration of responsibility for the management of his life. He will acknowledge his failures to act responsibly in so far

6   Ibid., para. 416

as he is aware of them; but he should know that his failures are partly rooted in deep-seated emotional disorders – such as excessive fear or anger or the undue craving to love and be loved – for which he is only slightly to blame. These powerful underground emotions cannot be mastered by an effort of will. They can only be rendered healthy and harmonious if relying on God he will co-operate with the self as it works to bring all its parts into order and harmony. He co-operates by confessing his weakness, his inability by his own efforts to control these passionate energies which threaten his aims. But he acknowledges his weakness with confidence that God, the Soul of his soul, will in time change his apparent enemies into allies.

(iv)

If confession is understood as the adoration of God by the individual in the awareness of the sin and evil in which he finds himself caught, thanksgiving can be seen as the acknowledgement of God in the awareness of the good and helpful factors in life. As in confession he will address God as an intimate inner Reality, responsive and caring, though infinitely transcending his understanding. In grateful dependence he will acknowledge as from God the mysterious force within him that makes for peace and health, the force that enables him to throw off illness, that fosters his well-being, both bodily and spiritual. Thanksgiving contradicts and counteracts the basic mistrust which infects mankind, estranges us from God and our fellows and hinders the development of our specifically human qualities. Thanksgiving acknowledges God's sustaining presence everywhere. One of the factors which militates against our growth in humanity is a tendency to get bogged down in the past, to cling to it for dear life and so to be hindered from grasping the opportunities and embracing the tasks of the present. We cling in nostalgia to a happiness or security we once enjoyed and long for its recovery. The over-age athlete looks back in memory to former triumphs and cannot wrench himself free to seek fulfilment in the present. Paradoxically we cling not only to good and happy memories but to painful and humiliating ones. Emotional wounds perhaps received in childhood, experiences of rejection, of loneliness, of thwarted rage or inconsolable grief, experiences so full of anguish as to be repressed and forgotten, live on in the unconscious like an invisible cancer, consuming psychic energy and sapping the individual's ability to face the present and the future. The practice of thanksgiving fosters a healthy detachment from, a letting go of the past; for it links past experience to the present reality of God. It might be thought that this would work well enough with happy experiences and memories but that it would not help a person to shake off the effects of the painful traumas of the past. No doubt it might require the expert help of the psychotherapist to enable an individual to recall deeply repressed memories. But where the individual has a genuine faith the painful wounds of the past once recalled can be healed by thanksgiving. For thanksgiving declares the believer's faith in God's infinitely resourceful presence even within evil, mitigating its effects and bringing good out of it. Indeed the power of God to redeem and draw good out of evil is at the very heart of the gospel. For the good news proclaims Christ's death on the cross, a deed of manifest and cruel injustice, to be the source of immeasurable blessings. Thanksgiving cannot of course change the past; but it can change its effects, through faith and memory working together, by bringing the past into the present of God, where old wounds can be healed and life imprisoned can be set free. Indeed the Eucharist, the principal act of Christian worship, draws its name from the central thanksgiving prayer, the prayer of consecration, which recalls in memory and celebrates in gratitude, over the symbols of bread and wine, the divine acts of creation and redemption, and so, as it were, brings the past across the centuries into the present.

In a different manner the prayer of petition fosters the same spirit of trust and openness towards God and one's fellows as well as to the deeps of one's own personality that thanksgiving encourages. It must be admitted that much petitionary prayer is childish and superstitious. It will therefore be in place to summarize in brief a theological view of petitionary prayer. St Thomas Aquinas gives two reasons for petition to God: to co-operate with divine providence and to awaken our confidence in him. Prayer is not a means of persuading God to do our will but the offering of heart and mind to God to be made the instrument of his. Just as an individual may become an agent of God's mercy by visiting the sick or feeding the hungry, so by his petitions he seeks to become the channel through which the waters of divine grace will flow. If it be asked why prayer should be needed to release the flow of God's lovingkindness, the answer is bound up with the nature of human freedom. Our freedom is a delicate plant which God is deeply concerned to foster, and such help as he gives will be of a kind to encourage and not hinder the growth of our humanity of which free will is an integral part. Petition when made with confidence and a genuine commitment to God's will does, I believe, open up the psychic channels in the one who prays, clogged as they usually are by the general mistrust, along which the life-enhancing waters of divine grace can flow.

So much for the theory of petitionary prayer. Can psychology shed light on some of the human factors at work in it? Aquinas refers to the subjective effect of petition upon the one who prays. To ask for things is typical of the child's attitude to the parents who love him and on whom he depends. Though we grow out of many childish attitudes, in every adult there lives a child or a set of buried tendencies typical of a child. Jung speaks of this childlike thing in an individual as the child archetype, an inherited tendency which circumstances such as surround childhood call into activity. The prayer of petition activates this child archetype and so brings into our approach to God an area of our being outside our conscious control. It is this archetypal tendency which leads people who are not in the habit of praying to call on their Maker in times of acute emergency or disaster. For the believer it is a wholly natural instinct to express his dependence upon and trust in a Power able and willing to help. Taught by Jung he will turn to a Presence within his own depths and seek to open himself more completely to the divine influence from within. Trust in God can be a deeper, fuller and more rationally grounded trust than the natural confidence in one's own inner resources. It would appear that immense resources for tackling problems and difficulties are locked up within our own being if only they could be made available; confident petition is a key which can unlock the door that shuts them in.

I have spoken of petitionary prayer as a means of opening ourselves to the inflow of divine grace. The same principle applies in intercession, prayer for others. It seems highly probable that telepathy is a factor present in intercession. The evidence for telepathy advanced by such investigators as Professor Rhine in the USA and Professor Vasiliev in Russia is so overwhelmingly strong that few doubt it, though perhaps only a few realize its significance for intercessory prayer. The phenomenon of telepathy seems to imply a constant interaction and interpenetration between people independent of spatial proximity. It appears that mind flows into mind, that images, feelings, ideas, flow from one person to another below the level of consciousness. The fact of telepathy lends support to Jung's belief in the collective unconscious of the human race. But it also lends support to the conviction that the prayers of one individual may be a means of blessing to many; that if one person opens himself up to the flow of divine grace, that flow will inevitably spread to many.

(v)

I have tried to show how Jung's teaching about the psyche can illuminate for the Christian the traditional fourfold approach to God in prayer. There are some further valuable lessons to be learnt from the method of active imagination which he encouraged his patients to use. Jung used to tell his patients to write down, reflect upon and sometimes to paint their dreams. The purpose of this is to bring about a healthy interaction between the conscious individual and his unconscious depths. The effect on the individual is to enlarge his consciousness by admitting into it some of the feelings and ideas from the unconscious. He also encouraged waking fantasies in which the individual in a relaxed and receptive attitude paid attention to the images which passed across the screen of the imagination. Sometimes the individual would have an imaginary dialogue with a figure on the screen, asking it questions and waiting for his imagination to throw up the answers. This practice of active imagination, as Jung called the exercise, may at first sight seem like playing a game of chess with yourself. But it can in fact be a valuable means of encouraging the conscious person to confront and come to terms with hitherto unconscious elements of his personality.

An old and well-tried method of imaginative reflection or meditation on some incident of the gospel narrative is remarkably similar to Jung's active imagination. You are encouraged in this method to read through the gospel narrative and picture its events as vividly as you can. You are to see with the eye of the imagination the various people described, to hear their words, to listen to the background noises. Then you proceed to question one of the people and hear in your imagination what he says in reply. No doubt the exercise is partly designed to bring a sense of historic actuality to the gospel story. But the meditation is a prelude to prayer and the imagined picture of Christ helps to make vivid to the individual his unseen presence. Imagination is made the servant of faith. The central figure in the pictured incident is Christ, the other figures help to make the imagined Christ real by the way they respond to him. To look at this from the standpoint of Jungian psychology, the Christ symbol stirs deep-seated archetypal tendencies into action. But the individual in his prayer looks through or away from his picture of Christ, which he knows, or should know, to be extremely inadequate and unworthy, to the unseen and unimaginable Godhead to which the Christ picture points. The value of this kind of imaginative reflection is partly that of Jung's active imagination; it brings into the light of consciousness ideas, feelings, attitudes which lie below the level of his ordinary awareness. But the believer's faith that in responding to Christ he is responding to God himself could mean that the exercise brings about a reciprocal interaction between the believer and his own deep centre, the integrating focus within the personality, the centre where God is most surely to be found.

This interaction between the conscious individual and the deep centre of his personality occurs at a profound level in the prayer of contemplation referred to briefly in Chapter 3. I will draw this chapter to a close with some comments on the human factor in this kind of prayer.[7] In contemplation the individual stops active thinking, reasoning and picturing in order to be open and receptive to God. The prayer is a silent waiting, a looking towards a Presence believed in intensely but not seen. It has been called a prayer of loving attention. The author of *The Cloud of Unknowing* describes it as a blind heaving up of the soul towards a cloud of unknowing. He writes: 'Strike that thick cloud of unknowing with the sharp dart of longing love.' A number of techniques, such as the repetition of a mantra, can assist the individual to still the active mind and to become open and receptive to ideas and impressions from within. But the spiritual guides are insistent that genuine contemplation is a gift from God which can be prepared for but cannot be commanded. It would seem that this contemplative waiting is only possible to one who is strongly committed to God. Contemplation can be likened to a flame burning in the heart, a flame of aspiration towards God in love and trust. In Jungian terms the child archetype is awakened into activity and with it a spirit of childlike trust that springs spontaneously from the depths of the personality.

The regular practice of prolonged waiting on God in contemplation slowly but surely transforms the individual. It is no easy process of change but is fraught with crises. For a change in the seat of control within the personality takes place. The individual normally learns with much effort to control his unruly desires and impulses with the help of a consciously held ideal of behaviour. The passive, receptive attitude of mind required in contemplation draws psychic energy away from this policing force and so allows repressed feelings and urges to become conscious in the form of powerful temptations to doubt, anger, fear, sloth or erotic fantasy. This is apt to be disconcerting for one intent on growing into closer union with God. What is required is a steadfastness which neither abandons itself to the lawless emotions and impulses

7 In my *River Within* (DLT 1978), ch. 8, I have given a fuller account of contemplative prayer

nor tries to get rid of them, but rather clings on to God by faith. The individual who stands firm in the midst of this psychic storm discovers that it changes its character. A new centre of control within him seems to take charge of these powerful energies and they cease to be threatening. A process of growing integration is taking place within the personality around a new centre. Gradually repressed or unrealized elements of the personality rise threateningly into consciousness and are slowly and not without a struggle brought under the sway of the centre. Each of these bits of the individual once it is owned and accepted brings an accession of strength. He feels himself grow freer, inwardly bigger, more himself. This is a psychological account of the kind of change that the regular practice of contemplation leads to. Jung would insist that this change cannot come about without the active participation of the conscious person. We can understand the transformation of the personality as a part of the God-created individuation process which Jung has described.

It is easy to see why spiritual writers are insistent on the dangers of this kind of waiting upon God for those insufficiently prepared for it. A certain strength and steadfastness is needed in the individual if he is to face and profit by the surge of archetypal energy that will force its way into his consciousness. Like an inexpert canoeist he may easily be capsized or carried away by the torrential waters on which he has ventured out. The spiritual writers, equally understandably, all insist on the need of an experienced spiritual guide for those who tread the way of contemplation. But if they speak of the dangers they are even more emphatic about the rewards of a life of growing union with God.

Prayer is a mysterious activity, involving as it does the human individual, whose personality reaches into unknown depths and heights in a responsive relationship with the greater Unknown of the Godhead. Jung, whose life-work was the exploration of the human psyche and for whom God was a central experience of his life, has, I believe, much to teach those who wish to embark upon the journey into God.

EPILOGUE

THE TRUTH OF WHAT YOU ARE

'What is man that thou art mindful of him: and the son of man that thou visitest him?' sings the psalmist, addressing his Maker. 'What a piece of work is man, how noble in reason, how infinite in faculty' muses Shakespeare, man of the Renaissance, in the person of Hamlet. Jung's life-work was the exploration of the mystery of man. But what especially concerned him was not so much humanity in general, those qualities shared by all the human race, but the unique human individual. He contrasted the *knowledge* obtainable from the scientific study of men and women based largely on statistics and the *understanding* of human individuals. The statistical average man or woman is an abstraction, and every actual human being is an exception to it. It is the unique qualities by which each individual differs from the average that make him significant. And so, though he acknowledges the usefulness of this scientific knowledge, he writes:

> If I want to understand an individual human being, I must lay aside all scientific knowledge of the average man and discard all theories in order to adopt a completely new and unprejudiced attitude. I can only approach the task of *understanding* with a free and open mind, whereas *knowledge*

of man, or insight into human character, presupposes all sorts of knowledge about mankind in general.[1]

In his lectures and writings as well as in his therapeutic work he laboured to help individuals to let go of the fears which were inhibiting their growth as human beings so that they might become fully themselves. Our social nature makes us unavoidably dependent on others, for only their appreciation and acceptance of us gives us the confidence to follow our own path. He helped individuals to break away from excessive dependence on the expectations of society in order to realize their own uniqueness and to discover and follow their own individual way.

As he reflected after the war on the condition of Europe and the world and the problems that met him in the men and women who came to him in his consulting room, he became oppressed by the danger to the individual of his being swallowed up by the collective. The development of large-scale industry, of vast commercial consortiums, of the large civil services which the modern state requires, tended to put a premium on conformity and obedience and to belittle the individual. The employees of these giant organizations felt themselves to be like interchangeable cogs in an impersonal machine. Jung feared that the undermining of the individual would create the psychological conditions in which men and women would accept a dictator and a totalitarian state with relief. From the vantage point of nearby Switzerland he had witnessed this taking place in pre-war Germany. He was convinced that the only force strong enough to enable the individual to withstand the pressure of society was religion. He writes:

> Just as man, as a social being, cannot in the long run exist without a tie to the community, so the individual will never find the real justification for his existence and his own spiritual and moral autonomy anywhere except in an extra-mundane principle capable of relativizing the overpowering influence of external factors. The individual who is not anchored in God can offer no resistance on his own

1   C.W., vol. x, para. 495

resources to the physical and moral blandishments of the world. For this he needs the evidence of inner transcendent experience which alone can protect him from the otherwise inevitable submersion in the mass. Merely intellectual or even moral insight into the stultification and moral irresponsibility of the mass man is a negative recognition and amounts to not much more than a wavering on the road to the atomization of the individual. It lacks the driving force of religious conviction, since it is merely rational.[2]

It was not religious practice such as church-going or acceptance of a creed that would protect the individual from being overpowered by the tyranny of the masses and enable him to maintain freedom and autonomy, but a personal relationship to God involving him in depth:

It is not ethical principles however lofty or creeds however orthodox that lay the foundations for the freedom and autonomy of the individual, but simply and solely the empirical awareness, the incontrovertible experience of an intensely personal, reciprocal relationship between man and an extra-mundane authority which acts as a counterpoise to the 'world' and its 'reason'.[3]

As I have said earlier, I think that Jung did not fully understand the place of dogma and creed in the Christian life. He seemed to understand the creed as a set of intellectual formulations unrelated to the inner life of the believer. No doubt this would describe the place of the creed in the lives of many professing Christians. But the creed is in reality a set of symbols referring to a transcendent Authority and a means of opening the believer to the divine Reality of which it speaks. The creed provides guidelines for worship as the opening words of the so-called Athanasian creed implies. 'This is the catholic faith that we *worship* one God in trinity and trinity in unity.' Believing properly means worshipping.

This book has tried to show that Christians have much to learn from the writings of Jung. But I believe that discussions between Christian theologians and Jungian experts would

2   Ibid., para. 511
3   Ibid., para. 509

discover a great deal more. The technical terms of Christian theology such as, for example, original sin or the atonement, despite the fact that they signify experienced spiritual reality, are apt to seem unreal even to many Christians today. Jung is able to illuminate this reality from the dreams of his patients as well as from the myths and fairy tales of mankind. He can help to bring dead-seeming doctrine to life and contemporary relevance. Would not the abstract idea of grace, which refers to the many and diverse ways in which the lovingkindness of God touches, heals and renews men and women, be illuminated by the idea of the archetype of the child, the inborn tendency for a childlike response to be roused in the face of presences and powers greater than ourselves? Preachers have spoken of Christ being born in us as well as in Bethlehem. Could Jung teach us to see this not just as a pious metaphor but as a powerful psychic reality? The study of the Bible might be transformed if we could understand the biblical images, not as poetical ways of stating what could with greater precision be stated in exact prose, but rather as powerful symbols able to release a flow of spiritual life in us, if only we will take them seriously and through imaginative reflection open ourselves to their impact.

Looking back on what I have written I am conscious of the inadequacy, the flatness, of the over-simplified account I have tried to give of some of Jung's explorations and discoveries in hitherto largely unknown regions of the human psyche. Any attempt to explain the complex and powerfully suggestive ideas of Jung almost inevitably involves some reduction and taming of their force, a force which can only be realized by studying and pondering Jung's own writings. I hope that what I have written will encourage readers to read or re-read Jung for themselves.

Some readers, both Christian and non-Christian, may criticize the way I have used Jung's ideas to buttress a personal view of Christianity. However, actual Christianity, which must include both Roman Catholics and Quakers, Eastern Orthodox and Salvation Army and a host of other sects and denominations, is so pluriform that to have described it adequately would have required another book. I have therefore thought it best to describe my own personal belief, which is that of an Anglican who is both loyal to the traditions of his Church and open to new ideas from whatever source. One of the truths that Jung has brought home to me is that the search for individuation, for wholeness, is in no way incompatible with but is rather complementary to the quest for union with God. This is not a new truth. Irenaeus stated it in a different way many centuries ago in his often quoted words, 'The glory of God is man fully alive'. But the coinage in which ancient truth was expressed needs to be minted anew if it is to circulate freely in the world of the late twentieth century. Jung's twentieth-century voice brings this truth home with a wealth of illustration; and I believe he can be of unique service to Christian pastors in this age of religious pluralism, when truth must be experienced if it is to be believed.

Recommended for Further Reading

Jung, Carl Gustav, et al. *Man and His Symbols.* New York: Dell, 1968
———. *Memories, Dreams and Reflections,* edited by Aniella Jaffe, translated by Richard Winston and Clara Winston. New York: Pantheon, 1963.
———. *Modern Man in Search of a Soul.* New York: Harcourt Brace Jovanovich, 1955.
Fordham, Frieda. *An Introduction to Jung's Psychology.* New York: Penguin Books, 1953.